TABLE OF CONTENTS

Sections:		Day:
1.	Adding Digits 0 - 5	1 - 10
2.	Adding Digits 0 - 7	10 - 20
3.	Adding Digits 0 - 10	20 - 30
4.	Subtracting Digits 0 - 10	30 - 40
5.	Subtracting Digits 10 - 20	40 - 50
6.	Subtracting Digits 0 - 20	50 - 75
7.	Adding and Subtracting	75 - 100

1. 2 + 0	2. 2 + 4	3. 3 + 1	4. 2 + 3	5. 1 + 2	6. 0 + 0
7. 4 + 2	8. 1 + 4	9. 2 + 5	10. 1 + 3	11. 0 + 2	12. 4 + 1
13. 3 + 4	14. 3 + 2	15. 4 + 3	16. 2 + 2	17. 3 + 3	18. 1 + 0
19. 5 + 0	20. 5 + 2	21. 0 + 4	22. 5 + 5	23. 1 + 5	24. 2 + 1
25. 5 + 4	26. 3 + 5	27. 4 + 4	28. 5 + 1	29. 1 + 1	30. 5 + 3
31. 4 + 0	32. 0 + 5	33. 4 + 5	34. 0 + 1	35. 0 + 3	36. 3 + 0
37. 3 + 3	38. 3 + 2	39. 0 + 2	40. 0 + 5	41. 3 + 0	42. 3 + 1
43. 2 + 2	44. 4 + 3	45. 0 + 3	46. 2 + 5	47. 3 + 1	48. 1 + 0
49. 1 + 2	50. 4 + 4	51. 1 + 4	52. 4 + 5	53. 4 + 5	54. 5 + 2
55. 0 + 0	56. 5 + 5	57. 0 + 2	58. 3 + 3	59. 3 + 4	60. 4 + 3

1.   1
  + 3
	2. 3
	  + 4
		3. 5
		  + 2
			4. 4
			  + 1
				5. 0
				  + 1
					6. 2
					  + 4

7.   3
  + 3
	8. 1
	  + 4
		9. 2
		  + 5
			10. 0
			  + 3
				11. 4
				  + 2
					12. 5
					  + 3

13.   5
  + 4
	14. 1
	  + 2
		15. 3
		  + 5
			16. 4
			  + 3
				17. 5
				  + 0
					18. 4
					  + 5

19.   5
  + 5
	20. 5
	  + 1
		21. 2
		  + 0
			22. 2
			  + 1
				23. 1
				  + 1
					24. 4
					  + 4

25.   1
  + 0
	26. 3
	  + 1
		27. 0
		  + 2
			28. 3
			  + 2
				29. 2
				  + 3
					30. 1
					  + 5

31.   4
  + 0
	32. 3
	  + 0
		33. 0
		  + 4
			34. 2
			  + 2
				35. 0
				  + 0
					36. 0
					  + 5

37.   2
  + 2
	38. 1
	  + 2
		39. 4
		  + 3
			40. 3
			  + 1
				41. 4
				  + 5
					42. 3
					  + 0

43.   3
  + 1
	44. 5
	  + 0
		45. 2
		  + 5
			46. 3
			  + 1
				47. 4
				  + 3
					48. 4
					  + 4

49.   1
  + 3
	50. 0
	  + 1
		51. 0
		  + 3
			52. 5
			  + 5
				53. 4
				  + 1
					54. 0
					  + 4

55.   4
  + 2
	56. 5
	  + 2
		57. 2
		  + 1
			58. 3
			  + 5
				59. 0
				  + 1
					60. 0
					  + 1

1. 2 + 5	2. 5 + 0	3. 2 + 3	4. 3 + 1	5. 2 + 0	6. 1 + 2
7. 2 + 2	8. 3 + 5	9. 0 + 4	10. 4 + 1	11. 5 + 4	12. 5 + 5
13. 4 + 3	14. 4 + 4	15. 3 + 2	16. 0 + 3	17. 3 + 0	18. 1 + 4
19. 2 + 4	20. 0 + 1	21. 3 + 4	22. 1 + 1	23. 0 + 2	24. 5 + 1
25. 1 + 5	26. 1 + 3	27. 0 + 0	28. 2 + 1	29. 4 + 0	30. 1 + 0
31. 5 + 3	32. 4 + 2	33. 4 + 5	34. 5 + 2	35. 3 + 3	36. 0 + 5
37. 0 + 1	38. 1 + 2	39. 2 + 3	40. 2 + 4	41. 4 + 2	42. 2 + 4
43. 4 + 4	44. 1 + 3	45. 0 + 0	46. 3 + 4	47. 3 + 4	48. 2 + 2
49. 4 + 2	50. 2 + 5	51. 1 + 2	52. 2 + 4	53. 2 + 5	54. 3 + 5
55. 4 + 4	56. 0 + 2	57. 3 + 0	58. 1 + 3	59. 3 + 1	60. 1 + 4

1. 0 + 3	2. 2 + 2	3. 2 + 4	4. 5 + 0	5. 4 + 3	6. 4 + 4
7. 2 + 3	8. 1 + 3	9. 1 + 1	10. 2 + 1	11. 1 + 2	12. 1 + 4
13. 4 + 1	14. 4 + 0	15. 3 + 4	16. 3 + 3	17. 1 + 0	18. 0 + 1
19. 3 + 1	20. 0 + 5	21. 2 + 0	22. 3 + 0	23. 4 + 5	24. 5 + 5
25. 3 + 2	26. 4 + 2	27. 5 + 2	28. 5 + 1	29. 0 + 4	30. 0 + 2
31. 5 + 4	32. 5 + 3	33. 2 + 5	34. 0 + 0	35. 1 + 5	36. 3 + 5
37. 2 + 2	38. 5 + 5	39. 4 + 4	40. 3 + 2	41. 3 + 1	42. 1 + 1
43. 4 + 5	44. 1 + 1	45. 3 + 4	46. 2 + 5	47. 2 + 2	48. 2 + 3
49. 3 + 2	50. 3 + 2	51. 1 + 1	52. 4 + 4	53. 4 + 2	54. 0 + 1
55. 1 + 5	56. 3 + 0	57. 2 + 1	58. 4 + 2	59. 4 + 2	60. 2 + 5

1.   2
  + 1
	2. 4
	  + 2
		3. 1
		  + 2
			4. 1
			  + 0
				5. 2
				  + 4
					6. 3
					  + 1

7.   4
  + 4
	8. 1
	  + 4
		9. 4
		  + 1
			10. 0
			  + 1
				11. 2
				  + 0
					12. 1
					  + 5

13.   2
  + 3
	14. 2
	  + 2
		15. 4
		  + 0
			16. 5
			  + 5
				17. 4
				  + 5
					18. 5
					  + 4

19.   0
  + 5
	20. 5
	  + 1
		21. 2
		  + 5
			22. 3
			  + 2
				23. 3
				  + 4
					24. 1
					  + 3

25.   3
  + 5
	26. 0
	  + 4
		27. 5
		  + 3
			28. 5
			  + 2
				29. 4
				  + 3
					30. 1
					  + 1

31.   3
  + 3
	32. 3
	  + 0
		33. 5
		  + 0
			34. 0
			  + 3
				35. 0
				  + 2
					36. 0
					  + 0

37.   0
  + 1
	38. 1
	  + 3
		39. 2
		  + 2
			40. 0
			  + 1
				41. 0
				  + 3
					42. 2
					  + 1

43.   2
  + 4
	44. 0
	  + 4
		45. 3
		  + 4
			46. 3
			  + 1
				47. 0
				  + 2
					48. 1
					  + 4

49.   1
  + 0
	50. 2
	  + 4
		51. 2
		  + 3
			52. 3
			  + 3
				53. 4
				  + 4
					54. 0
					  + 4

55.   0
  + 3
	56. 1
	  + 1
		57. 1
		  + 1
			58. 0
			  + 0
				59. 2
				  + 4
					60. 2
					  + 5

1.   2
  + 3
	2. 4
	  + 3
		3. 1
		  + 0
			4. 0
			  + 2
				5. 0
				  + 0
					6. 3
					  + 0

7.   3
  + 3
	8. 0
	  + 1
		9. 4
		  + 4
			10. 2
			  + 1
				11. 4
				  + 1
					12. 5
					  + 3

13.   2
  + 4
	14. 3
	  + 5
		15. 3
		  + 2
			16. 3
			  + 1
				17. 3
				  + 4
					18. 1
					  + 4

19.   1
  + 1
	20. 5
	  + 2
		21. 1
		  + 2
			22. 2
			  + 0
				23. 0
				  + 3
					24. 5
					  + 0

25.   1
  + 3
	26. 5
	  + 4
		27. 5
		  + 5
			28. 4
			  + 2
				29. 4
				  + 0
					30. 2
					  + 2

31.   0
  + 5
	32. 2
	  + 5
		33. 5
		  + 1
			34. 1
			  + 5
				35. 4
				  + 5
					36. 0
					  + 4

37.   3
  + 4
	38. 2
	  + 4
		39. 3
		  + 1
			40. 1
			  + 3
				41. 5
				  + 1
					42. 2
					  + 5

43.   3
  + 3
	44. 0
	  + 1
		45. 3
		  + 3
			46. 4
			  + 2
				47. 0
				  + 4
					48. 4
					  + 0

49.   0
  + 5
	50. 2
	  + 2
		51. 3
		  + 2
			52. 3
			  + 3
				53. 1
				  + 2
					54. 1
					  + 1

55.   1
  + 3
	56. 0
	  + 1
		57. 1
		  + 4
			58. 1
			  + 0
				59. 3
				  + 3
					60. 1
					  + 4

1.   2
  + 1
	2. 0
	  + 3
		3. 4
		  + 5
			4. 4
			  + 4
				5. 3
				  + 5
					6. 1
					  + 1

7.   2
  + 4
	8. 2
	  + 5
		9. 4
		  + 1
			10. 1
			  + 2
				11. 2
				  + 3
					12. 0
					  + 4

13.   1
  + 3
	14. 5
	  + 3
		15. 4
		  + 3
			16. 3
			  + 4
				17. 2
				  + 2
					18. 5
					  + 0

19.   3
  + 0
	20. 4
	  + 2
		21. 3
		  + 2
			22. 5
			  + 1
				23. 0
				  + 2
					24. 5
					  + 2

25.   0
  + 5
	26. 3
	  + 3
		27. 1
		  + 0
			28. 1
			  + 5
				29. 3
				  + 1
					30. 5
					  + 4

31.   2
  + 0
	32. 0
	  + 1
		33. 4
		  + 0
			34. 1
			  + 4
				35. 0
				  + 0
					36. 5
					  + 5

37.   0
  + 4
	38. 1
	  + 4
		39. 4
		  + 3
			40. 4
			  + 0
				41. 2
				  + 5
					42. 1
					  + 5

43.   4
  + 2
	44. 1
	  + 2
		45. 0
		  + 1
			46. 1
			  + 0
				47. 0
				  + 5
					48. 2
					  + 3

49.   4
  + 4
	50. 2
	  + 4
		51. 1
		  + 1
			52. 3
			  + 0
				53. 4
				  + 4
					54. 3
					  + 0

55.   2
  + 0
	56. 2
	  + 2
		57. 1
		  + 3
			58. 5
			  + 1
				59. 2
				  + 3
					60. 1
					  + 4

4 + 3	3 + 0	4 + 2	2 + 2	1 + 3	4 + 1
2 + 3	2 + 1	3 + 2	5 + 5	3 + 5	2 + 0
1 + 2	0 + 4	5 + 4	1 + 1	2 + 5	3 + 1
4 + 0	4 + 4	5 + 3	3 + 4	1 + 4	2 + 4
1 + 5	5 + 2	0 + 0	0 + 3	0 + 1	4 + 5
0 + 5	0 + 2	3 + 3	5 + 1	5 + 0	1 + 0
3 + 2	2 + 4	1 + 0	1 + 1	3 + 1	1 + 4
3 + 1	3 + 0	5 + 5	3 + 1	3 + 3	2 + 3
2 + 3	2 + 2	3 + 4	3 + 4	5 + 1	4 + 3
1 + 2	2 + 3	5 + 3	2 + 0	3 + 5	4 + 4

1 + 5	0 + 4	2 + 0	1 + 1	1 + 0	4 + 4
3 + 4	4 + 0	3 + 3	4 + 2	3 + 1	5 + 1
3 + 0	2 + 2	4 + 5	4 + 3	2 + 4	5 + 4
4 + 1	1 + 4	5 + 5	3 + 5	2 + 3	0 + 1
0 + 5	5 + 0	5 + 2	2 + 5	1 + 3	1 + 2
5 + 3	3 + 2	0 + 2	2 + 1	0 + 3	0 + 0
4 + 4	2 + 2	3 + 3	4 + 3	5 + 3	0 + 1
2 + 1	0 + 2	4 + 2	4 + 3	3 + 1	4 + 4
2 + 3	1 + 1	2 + 1	1 + 2	1 + 4	5 + 3
3 + 5	2 + 3	2 + 1	1 + 2	3 + 1	0 + 4

3 + 3	2 + 0	4 + 2	2 + 4	2 + 3	5 + 0
1 + 5	1 + 3	0 + 4	1 + 2	0 + 3	1 + 0
5 + 3	2 + 2	3 + 1	5 + 1	2 + 5	2 + 1
1 + 1	4 + 4	3 + 2	4 + 1	3 + 0	0 + 5
0 + 1	4 + 3	3 + 5	1 + 4	3 + 4	5 + 2
4 + 0	4 + 5	5 + 5	5 + 4	0 + 0	0 + 2
2 + 3	4 + 3	3 + 2	2 + 2	5 + 4	3 + 1
4 + 3	3 + 4	3 + 3	0 + 5	4 + 5	2 + 1
1 + 1	3 + 5	5 + 5	1 + 4	1 + 4	4 + 4
1 + 5	3 + 3	1 + 2	2 + 2	1 + 4	4 + 1

3 + 1	2 + 1	5 + 0	1 + 1	6 + 5	4 + 3
5 + 6	0 + 3	0 + 5	2 + 5	3 + 6	6 + 4
6 + 6	5 + 4	4 + 0	4 + 6	2 + 2	2 + 3
2 + 0	6 + 1	5 + 2	5 + 7	4 + 2	7 + 3
3 + 4	2 + 6	2 + 4	3 + 2	4 + 5	1 + 4
6 + 2	1 + 5	0 + 1	1 + 3	5 + 3	0 + 2
1 + 2	4 + 1	4 + 7	5 + 5	3 + 0	4 + 4
3 + 3	5 + 1	0 + 7	7 + 5	0 + 6	6 + 3
0 + 4	3 + 5	7 + 1	3 + 7	6 + 7	7 + 6
1 + 6	2 + 7	6 + 0	7 + 2	1 + 0	1 + 7

2 + 3	4 + 5	5 + 4	6 + 4	0 + 4	3 + 4
0 + 7	1 + 2	1 + 5	7 + 6	6 + 1	5 + 6
4 + 6	7 + 4	7 + 3	3 + 5	4 + 4	4 + 3
1 + 3	7 + 0	6 + 6	6 + 0	0 + 3	2 + 2
0 + 0	2 + 1	5 + 3	4 + 1	1 + 1	2 + 4
4 + 7	6 + 5	6 + 2	2 + 6	1 + 4	3 + 3
0 + 2	5 + 7	4 + 0	3 + 7	2 + 5	5 + 5
7 + 2	0 + 1	5 + 0	0 + 5	3 + 2	3 + 6
5 + 1	1 + 0	4 + 2	5 + 2	0 + 6	1 + 6
6 + 7	2 + 0	7 + 5	7 + 1	1 + 7	7 + 7

0 + 3	3 + 3	1 + 6	6 + 5	2 + 4	6 + 0
5 + 6	4 + 2	0 + 4	2 + 3	5 + 0	7 + 6
3 + 4	1 + 5	2 + 0	2 + 5	4 + 5	5 + 2
3 + 1	6 + 2	6 + 1	0 + 1	5 + 3	3 + 5
7 + 4	3 + 2	2 + 1	5 + 1	2 + 6	3 + 7
6 + 7	5 + 7	2 + 2	5 + 4	0 + 6	7 + 5
6 + 6	1 + 1	4 + 1	6 + 3	4 + 6	1 + 7
0 + 5	2 + 7	1 + 4	1 + 0	4 + 3	4 + 0
3 + 6	7 + 2	6 + 4	1 + 2	4 + 4	5 + 5
7 + 1	7 + 3	7 + 7	4 + 7	0 + 0	1 + 3

0 + 3	3 + 3	1 + 6	6 + 5	2 + 4	6 + 0
5 + 6	4 + 2	0 + 4	2 + 3	5 + 0	7 + 6
3 + 4	1 + 5	2 + 0	2 + 5	4 + 5	5 + 2
3 + 1	6 + 2	6 + 1	0 + 1	5 + 3	3 + 5
7 + 4	3 + 2	2 + 1	5 + 1	2 + 6	3 + 7
6 + 7	5 + 7	2 + 2	5 + 4	0 + 6	7 + 5
6 + 6	1 + 1	4 + 1	6 + 3	4 + 6	1 + 7
0 + 5	2 + 7	1 + 4	1 + 0	4 + 3	4 + 0
3 + 6	7 + 2	6 + 4	1 + 2	4 + 4	5 + 5
7 + 1	7 + 3	7 + 7	4 + 7	0 + 0	1 + 3

0 + 2	1 + 2	2 + 5	4 + 6	5 + 1	5 + 6
7 + 2	3 + 3	2 + 2	1 + 4	7 + 5	2 + 0
3 + 7	1 + 1	4 + 1	1 + 6	2 + 3	4 + 7
5 + 3	1 + 5	6 + 5	3 + 5	0 + 3	0 + 0
6 + 6	6 + 1	5 + 2	7 + 7	1 + 3	1 + 7
6 + 4	5 + 5	6 + 7	4 + 5	4 + 0	7 + 1
3 + 1	5 + 7	2 + 6	1 + 0	3 + 6	3 + 4
4 + 2	5 + 4	0 + 4	3 + 2	4 + 4	2 + 4
6 + 2	0 + 1	0 + 7	4 + 3	2 + 7	6 + 3
3 + 0	5 + 0	7 + 6	0 + 6	7 + 4	7 + 3

3 + 2	4 + 2	5 + 3	2 + 1	5 + 1	4 + 0
2 + 6	4 + 6	6 + 2	3 + 5	5 + 6	7 + 6
2 + 2	6 + 3	6 + 1	3 + 6	1 + 5	4 + 4
4 + 5	1 + 1	2 + 0	7 + 3	0 + 1	3 + 4
2 + 5	1 + 0	1 + 3	4 + 3	7 + 1	1 + 7
0 + 4	2 + 3	1 + 6	5 + 7	6 + 6	5 + 5
1 + 2	3 + 3	1 + 4	4 + 7	7 + 4	2 + 4
3 + 0	5 + 4	5 + 0	0 + 6	3 + 1	6 + 5
2 + 7	6 + 7	0 + 3	3 + 7	7 + 7	0 + 0
0 + 2	0 + 5	0 + 7	6 + 0	6 + 4	4 + 1

3 + 7	4 + 1	6 + 2	7 + 1	7 + 6	2 + 7
3 + 3	0 + 1	3 + 6	1 + 5	1 + 0	0 + 5
2 + 2	7 + 5	6 + 0	5 + 6	2 + 3	5 + 1
6 + 7	2 + 0	7 + 3	5 + 2	6 + 6	6 + 4
1 + 1	2 + 4	1 + 4	3 + 1	3 + 2	6 + 5
5 + 7	2 + 5	1 + 7	4 + 6	6 + 1	1 + 2
0 + 6	4 + 3	1 + 6	4 + 5	4 + 4	6 + 3
1 + 3	2 + 1	3 + 0	7 + 2	0 + 0	3 + 5
5 + 5	5 + 3	3 + 4	7 + 7	5 + 4	0 + 2
2 + 6	7 + 0	4 + 0	4 + 2	4 + 7	0 + 4

1 + 2	5 + 0	4 + 4	6 + 2	7 + 4	3 + 2
3 + 0	6 + 7	6 + 3	2 + 1	2 + 4	7 + 2
1 + 3	3 + 3	4 + 2	3 + 6	5 + 3	6 + 6
0 + 2	5 + 4	1 + 4	3 + 7	0 + 1	2 + 6
1 + 0	5 + 1	4 + 7	2 + 3	0 + 0	3 + 4
0 + 4	7 + 5	3 + 1	6 + 4	1 + 1	5 + 5
4 + 3	5 + 6	2 + 0	1 + 6	7 + 1	6 + 5
4 + 6	0 + 3	7 + 7	4 + 5	0 + 5	1 + 5
6 + 1	5 + 2	2 + 5	7 + 3	0 + 7	2 + 2
0 + 6	3 + 5	6 + 0	4 + 1	4 + 0	1 + 7

4 + 5	6 + 7	1 + 5	3 + 1	7 + 0	5 + 6
2 + 7	1 + 2	5 + 0	2 + 3	2 + 2	5 + 5
5 + 2	0 + 6	2 + 5	4 + 0	6 + 6	5 + 4
4 + 7	0 + 3	6 + 5	0 + 1	7 + 5	6 + 1
2 + 1	6 + 0	3 + 0	3 + 6	3 + 4	0 + 5
5 + 7	2 + 0	7 + 3	7 + 6	0 + 2	2 + 6
6 + 3	3 + 5	5 + 3	2 + 4	5 + 1	1 + 4
1 + 6	3 + 2	4 + 4	1 + 0	4 + 6	6 + 4
4 + 1	1 + 1	4 + 2	7 + 2	1 + 3	3 + 7
1 + 7	7 + 4	7 + 1	4 + 3	3 + 3	7 + 7

2 + 4	3 + 1	7 + 1	7 + 6	5 + 6	0 + 4
4 + 3	1 + 4	3 + 6	1 + 0	4 + 6	6 + 6
5 + 5	6 + 3	1 + 6	6 + 1	1 + 5	0 + 1
3 + 3	4 + 4	3 + 4	4 + 1	6 + 2	2 + 1
3 + 2	3 + 5	4 + 5	5 + 4	7 + 7	3 + 0
4 + 7	2 + 5	4 + 2	2 + 6	1 + 7	5 + 2
1 + 3	5 + 1	5 + 3	0 + 3	0 + 5	5 + 0
6 + 5	0 + 6	1 + 1	5 + 7	3 + 7	6 + 4
1 + 2	2 + 3	2 + 7	7 + 0	2 + 2	0 + 0
7 + 2	0 + 2	6 + 7	2 + 0	7 + 5	7 + 4

5 + 2	6 + 7	9 + 4	0 + 4	7 + 9	6 + 9
6 + 4	4 + 0	10 + 4	1 + 5	2 + 1	2 + 7
8 + 1	9 + 0	8 + 4	10 + 7	5 + 4	4 + 1
9 + 10	7 + 4	6 + 2	7 + 5	2 + 6	2 + 0
0 + 5	5 + 7	1 + 7	4 + 9	5 + 1	8 + 8
5 + 9	3 + 8	5 + 3	4 + 4	9 + 1	1 + 9
7 + 0	9 + 3	5 + 0	5 + 10	7 + 1	1 + 8
6 + 8	6 + 6	3 + 3	2 + 2	10 + 6	5 + 5
1 + 3	2 + 4	8 + 6	7 + 7	1 + 6	10 + 1
8 + 5	0 + 3	4 + 7	6 + 3	4 + 2	6 + 10

6 + 9	3 + 5	10 + 1	0 + 5	6 + 4	3 + 0
8 + 8	5 + 10	8 + 4	7 + 0	2 + 0	2 + 2
5 + 3	9 + 8	4 + 9	7 + 9	2 + 9	5 + 6
8 + 7	8 + 6	6 + 2	7 + 6	8 + 10	6 + 8
1 + 0	3 + 6	7 + 1	10 + 7	1 + 7	9 + 3
1 + 6	8 + 9	9 + 0	2 + 6	6 + 3	0 + 4
3 + 8	9 + 9	4 + 1	2 + 1	4 + 7	6 + 1
7 + 2	5 + 2	2 + 7	9 + 7	4 + 0	5 + 7
4 + 6	9 + 1	6 + 5	10 + 0	10 + 4	2 + 8
0 + 7	2 + 4	9 + 6	7 + 8	1 + 1	1 + 4

7 + 4	4 + 7	6 + 1	5 + 4	2 + 3	7 + 1
5 + 2	2 + 8	9 + 6	6 + 7	6 + 10	3 + 6
4 + 9	10 + 6	10 + 4	8 + 5	8 + 9	10 + 1
6 + 4	1 + 9	6 + 8	9 + 1	4 + 2	1 + 7
3 + 7	7 + 8	4 + 6	7 + 6	1 + 1	8 + 3
7 + 7	7 + 5	4 + 10	5 + 5	8 + 4	9 + 7
8 + 1	2 + 1	2 + 2	7 + 10	6 + 5	5 + 0
3 + 1	4 + 0	9 + 2	0 + 3	2 + 6	9 + 4
7 + 2	2 + 9	3 + 8	1 + 5	4 + 5	3 + 9
2 + 7	2 + 0	0 + 4	8 + 7	0 + 8	1 + 3

5 + 1	5 + 0	9 + 3	2 + 5	5 + 2	4 + 1
9 + 9	2 + 1	8 + 10	8 + 1	10 + 1	3 + 8
9 + 7	5 + 3	2 + 10	2 + 6	5 + 7	6 + 6
8 + 7	1 + 8	3 + 1	5 + 5	8 + 5	3 + 5
1 + 6	1 + 7	3 + 7	6 + 2	9 + 6	8 + 3
4 + 5	1 + 2	8 + 2	8 + 9	0 + 5	6 + 8
7 + 7	5 + 9	4 + 6	2 + 3	0 + 10	6 + 10
0 + 6	7 + 9	1 + 5	5 + 6	7 + 3	9 + 1
7 + 5	2 + 0	6 + 0	3 + 6	0 + 8	6 + 9
8 + 0	10 + 3	4 + 3	7 + 8	0 + 1	4 + 4

1 + 7	4 + 3	2 + 2	5 + 1	10 + 6	3 + 8
1 + 6	2 + 4	5 + 8	5 + 3	2 + 5	5 + 9
3 + 5	6 + 3	3 + 4	9 + 3	8 + 5	8 + 9
8 + 6	2 + 3	6 + 4	7 + 2	6 + 5	5 + 6
5 + 10	8 + 4	1 + 8	10 + 9	6 + 10	10 + 5
8 + 1	2 + 10	6 + 8	9 + 1	8 + 8	9 + 9
7 + 4	8 + 10	8 + 7	3 + 7	4 + 2	0 + 5
0 + 7	3 + 0	3 + 6	1 + 3	6 + 1	7 + 3
8 + 3	9 + 0	2 + 6	7 + 8	1 + 5	3 + 10
6 + 9	3 + 3	8 + 2	3 + 1	1 + 1	2 + 1

3 + 6	7 + 9	3 + 2	10 + 3	8 + 6	7 + 3
5 + 1	0 + 9	7 + 1	10 + 6	5 + 2	4 + 9
6 + 7	6 + 4	1 + 6	3 + 3	2 + 2	0 + 7
1 + 7	2 + 9	3 + 4	6 + 6	3 + 7	8 + 7
1 + 5	5 + 4	6 + 5	5 + 7	0 + 2	8 + 4
1 + 3	6 + 9	6 + 2	1 + 1	1 + 0	8 + 9
2 + 8	2 + 4	2 + 5	4 + 1	4 + 4	9 + 8
4 + 10	8 + 8	4 + 5	9 + 6	10 + 0	2 + 7
2 + 0	7 + 6	1 + 10	5 + 9	4 + 2	0 + 4
7 + 10	4 + 7	7 + 0	3 + 1	6 + 8	8 + 2

10 + 0	3 + 6	5 + 1	8 + 6	7 + 3	4 + 4
0 + 8	3 + 10	10 + 8	5 + 9	4 + 6	8 + 4
5 + 4	9 + 8	1 + 5	6 + 5	9 + 10	3 + 1
8 + 0	10 + 1	3 + 0	7 + 0	6 + 2	2 + 7
8 + 7	6 + 4	2 + 9	0 + 1	2 + 1	5 + 3
8 + 9	10 + 4	9 + 4	7 + 8	9 + 3	3 + 7
7 + 5	1 + 9	3 + 8	7 + 7	0 + 5	7 + 4
1 + 7	6 + 0	2 + 8	1 + 3	8 + 3	2 + 6
4 + 7	10 + 7	10 + 9	2 + 2	6 + 3	7 + 2
5 + 8	4 + 3	4 + 9	2 + 3	9 + 7	4 + 2

9 + 9	1 + 7	9 + 8	5 + 2	8 + 4	8 + 7
3 + 5	7 + 5	0 + 7	6 + 3	5 + 5	1 + 9
7 + 9	2 + 7	6 + 6	8 + 1	1 + 2	9 + 4
6 + 5	7 + 8	4 + 1	8 + 9	7 + 6	2 + 9
9 + 7	6 + 4	0 + 10	3 + 3	4 + 4	2 + 1
5 + 8	7 + 0	8 + 3	1 + 6	6 + 2	2 + 3
10 + 4	4 + 9	2 + 10	1 + 3	0 + 1	1 + 4
1 + 8	0 + 6	8 + 6	7 + 1	3 + 9	4 + 3
7 + 3	2 + 5	6 + 8	9 + 5	5 + 0	2 + 0
4 + 7	6 + 0	10 + 5	5 + 3	2 + 8	7 + 4

7 + 2	9 + 6	7 + 0	6 + 4	2 + 3	3 + 5
6 + 3	0 + 4	5 + 9	9 + 9	6 + 8	9 + 5
10 + 5	2 + 2	2 + 1	2 + 9	10 + 6	7 + 6
1 + 0	8 + 10	2 + 4	6 + 2	1 + 2	6 + 1
4 + 8	4 + 3	1 + 1	8 + 6	0 + 10	3 + 4
4 + 5	8 + 0	2 + 5	5 + 2	2 + 8	6 + 7
6 + 0	3 + 7	8 + 2	0 + 5	0 + 7	6 + 9
9 + 10	3 + 9	1 + 9	1 + 5	5 + 6	1 + 7
1 + 3	4 + 0	9 + 4	8 + 5	4 + 6	5 + 4
3 + 6	7 + 3	7 + 5	7 + 4	5 + 7	3 + 8

2 + 3	7 + 5	3 + 5	2 + 8	8 + 4	9 + 1
10 + 2	7 + 7	10 + 10	2 + 6	6 + 7	1 + 1
4 + 1	5 + 5	9 + 3	8 + 3	6 + 1	0 + 4
4 + 0	0 + 2	6 + 2	0 + 9	2 + 1	8 + 9
4 + 6	1 + 5	1 + 2	10 + 8	9 + 4	6 + 6
5 + 8	3 + 10	1 + 9	5 + 4	1 + 8	7 + 4
1 + 7	5 + 9	9 + 10	2 + 7	9 + 6	3 + 3
3 + 2	6 + 8	7 + 9	8 + 5	4 + 3	9 + 8
1 + 3	5 + 1	9 + 7	1 + 6	5 + 3	2 + 9
10 + 3	2 + 4	8 + 1	5 + 0	7 + 2	1 + 0

1. 1 − 1	2. 10 − 6	3. 9 − 4	4. 7 − 2	5. 4 − 4	6. 8 − 5
7. 7 − 4	8. 7 − 1	9. 4 − 3	10. 2 − 2	11. 9 − 1	12. 10 − 3
13. 8 − 7	14. 4 − 2	15. 1 − 0	16. 2 − 0	17. 3 − 1	18. 2 − 1
19. 10 − 7	20. 9 − 7	21. 5 − 4	22. 8 − 1	23. 4 − 1	24. 8 − 6
25. 9 − 9	26. 9 − 3	27. 10 − 2	28. 9 − 5	29. 8 − 4	30. 9 − 0
31. 5 − 5	32. 3 − 2	33. 5 − 0	34. 6 − 5	35. 7 − 0	36. 8 − 3
37. 6 − 2	38. 5 − 3	39. 5 − 2	40. 10 − 1	41. 6 − 6	42. 7 − 5
43. 6 − 3	44. 7 − 3	45. 8 − 2	46. 9 − 6	47. 6 − 4	48. 6 − 1
49. 5 − 1	50. 3 − 0	51. 9 − 8	52. 4 − 0	53. 10 − 5	54. 8 − 8
55. 7 − 6	56. 6 − 0	57. 7 − 7	58. 3 − 3	59. 8 − 0	60. 10 − 9

Day 32

Subtracting Digits 0 - 10

1. 8 − 1	2. 9 − 1	3. 8 − 4	4. 5 − 5	5. 7 − 6	6. 8 − 7
7. 5 − 1	8. 10 − 8	9. 7 − 5	10. 4 − 3	11. 10 − 2	12. 6 − 6
13. 7 − 3	14. 3 − 1	15. 6 − 5	16. 7 − 7	17. 7 − 0	18. 10 − 5
19. 7 − 4	20. 6 − 1	21. 10 − 3	22. 5 − 0	23. 10 − 6	24. 3 − 2
25. 4 − 2	26. 9 − 7	27. 8 − 6	28. 8 − 0	29. 2 − 0	30. 8 − 2
31. 3 − 3	32. 2 − 2	33. 10 − 10	34. 4 − 4	35. 9 − 9	36. 9 − 5
37. 10 − 4	38. 7 − 2	39. 10 − 0	40. 6 − 0	41. 1 − 1	42. 5 − 2
43. 9 − 2	44. 6 − 4	45. 6 − 2	46. 0 − 0	47. 5 − 3	48. 4 − 1
49. 9 − 3	50. 8 − 8	51. 10 − 1	52. 9 − 8	53. 8 − 3	54. 9 − 6
55. 4 − 0	56. 6 − 3	57. 2 − 1	58. 8 − 5	59. 7 − 1	60. 10 − 9

1. 9 − 8	2. 7 − 4	3. 8 − 2	4. 6 − 5	5. 8 − 4	6. 3 − 1
7. 5 − 3	8. 8 − 0	9. 10 − 6	10. 10 − 4	11. 4 − 3	12. 9 − 3
13. 2 − 0	14. 10 − 5	15. 8 − 6	16. 10 − 3	17. 9 − 5	18. 7 − 0
19. 6 − 1	20. 9 − 9	21. 10 − 9	22. 5 − 1	23. 2 − 2	24. 6 − 4
25. 9 − 2	26. 10 − 1	27. 3 − 0	28. 8 − 8	29. 9 − 6	30. 2 − 1
31. 5 − 2	32. 8 − 7	33. 6 − 6	34. 8 − 5	35. 10 − 2	36. 9 − 0
37. 5 − 4	38. 5 − 5	39. 9 − 1	40. 9 − 7	41. 4 − 4	42. 3 − 2
43. 7 − 3	44. 7 − 2	45. 10 − 7	46. 5 − 0	47. 10 − 0	48. 8 − 1
49. 7 − 6	50. 7 − 1	51. 8 − 3	52. 6 − 3	53. 7 − 5	54. 6 − 2
55. 4 − 2	56. 9 − 4	57. 1 − 1	58. 7 − 7	59. 6 − 0	60. 10 − 8

1. 6 − 0	2. 5 − 4	3. 3 − 0	4. 7 − 6	5. 4 − 2	6. 9 − 6
7. 9 − 1	8. 3 − 1	9. 10 − 5	10. 8 − 2	11. 6 − 5	12. 7 − 1
13. 10 − 7	14. 9 − 9	15. 7 − 7	16. 1 − 1	17. 10 − 6	18. 2 − 2
19. 10 − 9	20. 5 − 2	21. 5 − 5	22. 4 − 1	23. 4 − 4	24. 8 − 0
25. 9 − 7	26. 6 − 1	27. 7 − 5	28. 10 − 1	29. 9 − 2	30. 10 − 2
31. 3 − 3	32. 5 − 3	33. 10 − 3	34. 9 − 5	35. 2 − 0	36. 8 − 6
37. 7 − 3	38. 4 − 0	39. 6 − 6	40. 1 − 0	41. 9 − 3	42. 8 − 4
43. 6 − 4	44. 7 − 4	45. 4 − 3	46. 6 − 3	47. 10 − 8	48. 10 − 10
49. 6 − 2	50. 8 − 1	51. 7 − 2	52. 2 − 1	53. 0 − 0	54. 9 − 0
55. 9 − 4	56. 8 − 8	57. 8 − 3	58. 8 − 7	59. 9 − 8	60. 8 − 5

1. 8
  − 1
	2. 3
	  − 2
		3. 7
		  − 6
			4. 5
			  − 5
				5. 9
				  − 6
					6. 6
					  − 1

7. 9
  − 4
	8. 8
	  − 2
		9. 4
		  − 3
			10. 7
			  − 2
				11. 8
				  − 8
					12. 5
					  − 2

13. 8
  − 3
	14. 5
	  − 1
		15. 8
		  − 7
			16. 7
			  − 1
				17. 4
				  − 1
					18. 4
					  − 4

19. 6
  − 5
	20. 4
	  − 2
		21. 4
		  − 0
			22. 9
			  − 8
				23. 9
				  − 1
					24. 6
					  − 2

25. 6
  − 3
	26. 3
	  − 3
		27. 9
		  − 7
			28. 1
			  − 0
				29. 9
				  − 9
					30. 10
					  − 5

31. 5
  − 3
	32. 9
	  − 5
		33. 6
		  − 6
			34. 9
			  − 3
				35. 8
				  − 5
					36. 7
					  − 4

37. 8
  − 4
	38. 6
	  − 0
		39. 7
		  − 7
			40. 3
			  − 0
				41. 7
				  − 0
					42. 8
					  − 6

43. 7
  − 3
	44. 2
	  − 0
		45. 3
		  − 1
			46. 2
			  − 1
				47. 2
				  − 2
					48. 9
					  − 2

49. 1
  − 1
	50. 10
	  − 8
		51. 10
		  − 4
			52. 10
			  − 7
				53. 10
				  − 1
					54. 7
					  − 5

55. 10
  − 6
	56. 5
	  − 4
		57. 6
		  − 4
			58. 10
			  − 0
				59. 10
				  − 9
					60. 5
					  − 0

1. 5 − 1	2. 8 − 1	3. 10 − 4	4. 7 − 3	5. 2 − 1	6. 8 − 2
7. 9 − 7	8. 10 − 9	9. 3 − 0	10. 10 − 8	11. 2 − 2	12. 10 − 5
13. 9 − 2	14. 9 − 5	15. 0 − 0	16. 7 − 1	17. 3 − 2	18. 4 − 3
19. 6 − 3	20. 7 − 4	21. 9 − 8	22. 7 − 6	23. 9 − 1	24. 9 − 6
25. 6 − 1	26. 3 − 3	27. 9 − 9	28. 10 − 7	29. 7 − 7	30. 10 − 2
31. 8 − 6	32. 1 − 0	33. 4 − 4	34. 10 − 6	35. 5 − 4	36. 9 − 3
37. 8 − 4	38. 3 − 1	39. 5 − 2	40. 4 − 2	41. 6 − 4	42. 8 − 3
43. 10 − 0	44. 9 − 0	45. 9 − 4	46. 4 − 1	47. 8 − 7	48. 7 − 5
49. 1 − 1	50. 6 − 5	51. 6 − 0	52. 7 − 0	53. 10 − 1	54. 2 − 0
55. 5 − 3	56. 8 − 5	57. 6 − 2	58. 5 − 5	59. 10 − 3	60. 7 − 2

1.   6
  − 2
	2. 9
	  − 7
		3. 3
		  − 2
			4. 6
			  − 0
				5. 6
				  − 4
					6. 0
					  − 0

7.   2
  − 2
	8. 8
	  − 8
		9. 9
		  − 3
			10. 6
			  − 3
				11. 7
				  − 4
					12. 5
					  − 1

13.   3
  − 3
	14. 9
	  − 8
		15. 8
		  − 0
			16. 7
			  − 3
				17. 10
				  − 4
					18. 8
					  − 6

19.   9
  − 5
	20. 1
	  − 0
		21. 7
		  − 5
			22. 8
			  − 4
				23. 7
				  − 7
					24. 8
					  − 3

25.   7
  − 6
	26. 3
	  − 0
		27. 9
		  − 9
			28. 6
			  − 5
				29. 8
				  − 2
					30. 8
					  − 5

31.   4
  − 3
	32. 1
	  − 1
		33. 4
		  − 4
			34. 9
			  − 2
				35. 8
				  − 1
					36. 2
					  − 1

37.   4
  − 2
	38. 5
	  − 4
		39. 5
		  − 3
			40. 6
			  − 6
				41. 6
				  − 1
					42. 4
					  − 1

43.   3
  − 1
	44. 5
	  − 5
		45. 2
		  − 0
			46. 9
			  − 1
				47. 10
				  − 8
					48. 10
					  − 1

49.   10
  − 5
	50. 7
	  − 1
		51. 10
		  − 3
			52. 8
			  − 7
				53. 5
				  − 2
					54. 7
					  − 2

55.   5
  − 0
	56. 9
	  − 4
		57. 10
		  − 2
			58. 4
			  − 0
				59. 9
				  − 6
					60. 10
					  − 6

1. 8 − 1	2. 8 − 3	3. 8 − 7	4. 2 − 2	5. 1 − 1	6. 9 − 1
7. 10 − 6	8. 5 − 3	9. 3 − 3	10. 9 − 5	11. 10 − 7	12. 7 − 5
13. 4 − 4	14. 8 − 2	15. 4 − 2	16. 7 − 7	17. 3 − 1	18. 8 − 5
19. 6 − 5	20. 2 − 1	21. 4 − 1	22. 5 − 5	23. 5 − 1	24. 9 − 7
25. 9 − 2	26. 9 − 6	27. 9 − 0	28. 7 − 3	29. 8 − 8	30. 4 − 3
31. 10 − 0	32. 9 − 9	33. 4 − 0	34. 8 − 4	35. 9 − 4	36. 9 − 8
37. 3 − 0	38. 6 − 3	39. 5 − 2	40. 6 − 6	41. 1 − 0	42. 10 − 4
43. 10 − 5	44. 6 − 4	45. 6 − 2	46. 10 − 10	47. 7 − 2	48. 7 − 1
49. 8 − 6	50. 10 − 8	51. 10 − 9	52. 9 − 3	53. 10 − 1	54. 7 − 0
55. 5 − 4	56. 6 − 1	57. 10 − 3	58. 5 − 0	59. 7 − 4	60. 2 − 0

1. 5 − 3	2. 10 − 5	3. 7 − 1	4. 8 − 5	5. 6 − 1	6. 8 − 0
7. 7 − 4	8. 8 − 1	9. 7 − 7	10. 6 − 5	11. 9 − 5	12. 4 − 3
13. 4 − 1	14. 8 − 6	15. 8 − 7	16. 10 − 2	17. 7 − 2	18. 10 − 1
19. 7 − 0	20. 8 − 4	21. 9 − 6	22. 9 − 7	23. 10 − 3	24. 2 − 2
25. 6 − 4	26. 3 − 2	27. 5 − 4	28. 4 − 4	29. 8 − 8	30. 1 − 1
31. 10 − 4	32. 2 − 1	33. 7 − 5	34. 5 − 5	35. 7 − 3	36. 1 − 0
37. 9 − 2	38. 3 − 0	39. 5 − 1	40. 6 − 3	41. 9 − 3	42. 6 − 2
43. 10 − 6	44. 7 − 6	45. 8 − 2	46. 5 − 2	47. 9 − 8	48. 4 − 0
49. 9 − 9	50. 3 − 3	51. 8 − 3	52. 9 − 1	53. 6 − 0	54. 2 − 0
55. 5 − 0	56. 9 − 4	57. 3 − 1	58. 6 − 6	59. 10 − 10	60. 10 − 8

1. 9 − 2	2. 1 − 1	3. 4 − 4	4. 6 − 1	5. 9 − 7	6. 9 − 5
7. 9 − 1	8. 5 − 1	9. 7 − 5	10. 9 − 3	11. 8 − 6	12. 7 − 6
13. 10 − 7	14. 2 − 1	15. 8 − 1	16. 7 − 2	17. 5 − 3	18. 6 − 4
19. 7 − 3	20. 10 − 4	21. 10 − 3	22. 3 − 3	23. 4 − 0	24. 5 − 5
25. 7 − 1	26. 4 − 1	27. 9 − 8	28. 9 − 6	29. 10 − 9	30. 2 − 0
31. 8 − 8	32. 6 − 2	33. 8 − 2	34. 7 − 4	35. 8 − 5	36. 4 − 3
37. 7 − 7	38. 4 − 2	39. 8 − 3	40. 5 − 2	41. 10 − 6	42. 1 − 0
43. 3 − 1	44. 3 − 2	45. 6 − 3	46. 9 − 9	47. 10 − 5	48. 10 − 2
49. 2 − 2	50. 10 − 1	51. 6 − 6	52. 5 − 4	53. 8 − 4	54. 7 − 0
55. 10 − 8	56. 6 − 5	57. 8 − 7	58. 6 − 0	59. 10 − 0	60. 9 − 4

1. 19 − 13	2. 19 − 18	3. 15 − 13	4. 16 − 13	5. 14 − 11	6. 16 − 12
7. 16 − 11	8. 14 − 13	9. 15 − 11	10. 19 − 17	11. 10 − 10	12. 19 − 15
13. 19 − 16	14. 20 − 19	15. 16 − 15	16. 19 − 14	17. 20 − 18	18. 18 − 16
19. 17 − 13	20. 11 − 11	21. 14 − 12	22. 18 − 15	23. 17 − 16	24. 20 − 20
25. 19 − 19	26. 13 − 13	27. 13 − 11	28. 17 − 12	29. 18 − 12	30. 15 − 15
31. 17 − 14	32. 14 − 10	33. 19 − 12	34. 16 − 16	35. 16 − 14	36. 15 − 14
37. 19 − 11	38. 20 − 16	39. 18 − 11	40. 20 − 11	41. 20 − 13	42. 13 − 10
43. 18 − 17	44. 17 − 17	45. 12 − 10	46. 18 − 18	47. 20 − 14	48. 12 − 12
49. 17 − 15	50. 18 − 14	51. 20 − 17	52. 15 − 10	53. 17 − 10	54. 18 − 10
55. 20 − 10	56. 11 − 10	57. 13 − 12	58. 14 − 14	59. 18 − 13	60. 19 − 10

1. 20 − 15	2. 17 − 16	3. 19 − 19	4. 20 − 18	5. 18 − 13	6. 14 − 12
7. 17 − 12	8. 17 − 14	9. 15 − 15	10. 11 − 11	11. 16 − 13	12. 17 − 15
13. 20 − 13	14. 19 − 11	15. 15 − 10	16. 19 − 17	17. 17 − 13	18. 12 − 11
19. 14 − 10	20. 15 − 12	21. 13 − 11	22. 15 − 14	23. 14 − 13	24. 18 − 17
25. 16 − 14	26. 20 − 19	27. 19 − 12	28. 16 − 16	29. 19 − 13	30. 17 − 17
31. 20 − 11	32. 13 − 10	33. 18 − 11	34. 15 − 13	35. 14 − 11	36. 19 − 16
37. 17 − 11	38. 19 − 14	39. 16 − 10	40. 13 − 12	41. 12 − 12	42. 11 − 10
43. 18 − 14	44. 20 − 14	45. 14 − 14	46. 16 − 12	47. 19 − 15	48. 15 − 11
49. 19 − 10	50. 10 − 10	51. 16 − 15	52. 20 − 16	53. 13 − 13	54. 16 − 11
55. 20 − 10	56. 18 − 16	57. 20 − 12	58. 20 − 17	59. 18 − 15	60. 18 − 12

1. 18 − 15	2. 17 − 14	3. 17 − 13	4. 13 − 10	5. 16 − 11	6. 12 − 12
7. 19 − 16	8. 17 − 11	9. 17 − 12	10. 15 − 11	11. 19 − 15	12. 18 − 16
13. 19 − 12	14. 15 − 10	15. 16 − 14	16. 17 − 15	17. 14 − 11	18. 19 − 19
19. 16 − 10	20. 16 − 16	21. 16 − 15	22. 20 − 18	23. 18 − 13	24. 15 − 14
25. 19 − 10	26. 18 − 18	27. 15 − 15	28. 13 − 11	29. 17 − 16	30. 17 − 10
31. 13 − 13	32. 18 − 12	33. 16 − 12	34. 18 − 14	35. 13 − 12	36. 12 − 10
37. 19 − 13	38. 11 − 11	39. 20 − 16	40. 19 − 14	41. 14 − 10	42. 14 − 14
43. 16 − 13	44. 12 − 11	45. 20 − 13	46. 15 − 13	47. 10 − 10	48. 18 − 17
49. 19 − 11	50. 17 − 17	51. 14 − 12	52. 20 − 15	53. 14 − 13	54. 19 − 18
55. 18 − 11	56. 19 − 17	57. 20 − 19	58. 15 − 12	59. 20 − 20	60. 20 − 17

1. 19 − 19	2. 20 − 13	3. 14 − 14	4. 20 − 15	5. 17 − 15	6. 13 − 13
7. 16 − 11	8. 19 − 13	9. 17 − 14	10. 13 − 11	11. 16 − 15	12. 16 − 13
13. 17 − 13	14. 18 − 16	15. 19 − 11	16. 18 − 13	17. 20 − 10	18. 17 − 12
19. 12 − 12	20. 15 − 10	21. 18 − 11	22. 16 − 16	23. 16 − 12	24. 16 − 10
25. 15 − 13	26. 19 − 16	27. 17 − 10	28. 20 − 19	29. 14 − 13	30. 19 − 17
31. 15 − 12	32. 19 − 10	33. 16 − 14	34. 13 − 10	35. 20 − 11	36. 12 − 10
37. 15 − 15	38. 20 − 12	39. 18 − 12	40. 11 − 11	41. 19 − 15	42. 13 − 12
43. 17 − 11	44. 20 − 14	45. 20 − 20	46. 18 − 15	47. 19 − 12	48. 18 − 17
49. 20 − 16	50. 15 − 11	51. 12 − 11	52. 17 − 17	53. 18 − 14	54. 14 − 12
55. 20 − 18	56. 14 − 11	57. 19 − 14	58. 15 − 14	59. 17 − 16	60. 20 − 17

1. 16 − 16	2. 19 − 15	3. 14 − 13	4. 16 − 11	5. 20 − 14	6. 15 − 11
7. 18 − 16	8. 16 − 10	9. 17 − 13	10. 15 − 14	11. 12 − 12	12. 18 − 15
13. 20 − 18	14. 15 − 13	15. 17 − 11	16. 19 − 16	17. 20 − 19	18. 15 − 10
19. 18 − 17	20. 14 − 10	21. 19 − 13	22. 19 − 11	23. 19 − 12	24. 18 − 11
25. 17 − 12	26. 13 − 11	27. 20 − 15	28. 20 − 13	29. 14 − 14	30. 19 − 14
31. 11 − 10	32. 16 − 15	33. 19 − 18	34. 20 − 17	35. 19 − 19	36. 18 − 14
37. 17 − 16	38. 17 − 10	39. 16 − 13	40. 20 − 11	41. 14 − 11	42. 13 − 13
43. 16 − 14	44. 14 − 12	45. 19 − 10	46. 17 − 17	47. 17 − 15	48. 15 − 15
49. 11 − 11	50. 17 − 14	51. 18 − 12	52. 20 − 12	53. 13 − 12	54. 18 − 10
55. 19 − 17	56. 15 − 12	57. 13 − 10	58. 18 − 13	59. 16 − 12	60. 12 − 11

1. 15 − 10	2. 12 − 12	3. 17 − 15	4. 16 − 12	5. 16 − 14	6. 14 − 13
7. 20 − 11	8. 11 − 11	9. 19 − 17	10. 18 − 17	11. 17 − 16	12. 12 − 11
13. 13 − 11	14. 19 − 12	15. 15 − 14	16. 16 − 13	17. 17 − 13	18. 18 − 11
19. 19 − 13	20. 20 − 14	21. 18 − 16	22. 13 − 10	23. 19 − 18	24. 18 − 15
25. 14 − 14	26. 15 − 15	27. 19 − 11	28. 18 − 18	29. 12 − 10	30. 20 − 12
31. 13 − 12	32. 19 − 14	33. 17 − 17	34. 17 − 12	35. 19 − 15	36. 20 − 19
37. 20 − 17	38. 14 − 12	39. 17 − 14	40. 15 − 12	41. 18 − 14	42. 20 − 18
43. 10 − 10	44. 18 − 13	45. 18 − 10	46. 18 − 12	47. 16 − 10	48. 16 − 16
49. 19 − 16	50. 14 − 11	51. 19 − 19	52. 20 − 16	53. 15 − 11	54. 17 − 11
55. 11 − 10	56. 16 − 11	57. 13 − 13	58. 14 − 10	59. 16 − 15	60. 19 − 10

1. 19 − 12	2. 13 − 11	3. 15 − 15	4. 18 − 12	5. 19 − 18	6. 12 − 11
7. 19 − 15	8. 14 − 13	9. 19 − 17	10. 16 − 12	11. 20 − 17	12. 19 − 16
13. 12 − 12	14. 11 − 10	15. 11 − 11	16. 18 − 13	17. 17 − 17	18. 18 − 15
19. 17 − 12	20. 14 − 11	21. 17 − 13	22. 17 − 15	23. 18 − 18	24. 16 − 10
25. 15 − 14	26. 17 − 11	27. 12 − 10	28. 18 − 16	29. 17 − 16	30. 15 − 12
31. 19 − 10	32. 17 − 10	33. 19 − 13	34. 13 − 13	35. 14 − 12	36. 18 − 14
37. 16 − 16	38. 18 − 11	39. 15 − 11	40. 14 − 14	41. 20 − 15	42. 16 − 15
43. 20 − 18	44. 13 − 12	45. 16 − 13	46. 14 − 10	47. 20 − 11	48. 20 − 12
49. 19 − 19	50. 20 − 19	51. 19 − 14	52. 15 − 13	53. 17 − 14	54. 16 − 11
55. 15 − 10	56. 20 − 13	57. 16 − 14	58. 20 − 14	59. 19 − 11	60. 18 − 17

1. 19 - 11	2. 20 - 19	3. 17 - 12	4. 16 - 14	5. 17 - 16	6. 17 - 11
7. 19 - 15	8. 17 - 17	9. 16 - 10	10. 20 - 16	11. 19 - 17	12. 14 - 13
13. 18 - 12	14. 16 - 12	15. 12 - 11	16. 19 - 14	17. 16 - 16	18. 10 - 10
19. 11 - 10	20. 17 - 14	21. 17 - 15	22. 15 - 11	23. 18 - 14	24. 12 - 10
25. 15 - 14	26. 18 - 15	27. 20 - 13	28. 13 - 13	29. 19 - 13	30. 16 - 11
31. 13 - 12	32. 18 - 13	33. 12 - 12	34. 18 - 16	35. 14 - 14	36. 20 - 20
37. 20 - 11	38. 15 - 15	39. 18 - 18	40. 15 - 13	41. 14 - 10	42. 18 - 17
43. 20 - 12	44. 20 - 17	45. 19 - 16	46. 11 - 11	47. 14 - 11	48. 13 - 11
49. 17 - 10	50. 15 - 10	51. 14 - 12	52. 16 - 15	53. 17 - 13	54. 19 - 12
55. 19 - 18	56. 20 - 18	57. 15 - 12	58. 16 - 13	59. 18 - 10	60. 13 - 10

NAME: _______________ TIME: _______ Score: /60

1. 12 − 10	2. 15 − 12	3. 19 − 11	4. 14 − 11	5. 17 − 14	6. 20 − 12
7. 18 − 12	8. 16 − 14	9. 18 − 11	10. 19 − 18	11. 19 − 13	12. 15 − 14
13. 14 − 14	14. 11 − 11	15. 18 − 13	16. 16 − 15	17. 17 − 15	18. 19 − 15
19. 15 − 13	20. 15 − 11	21. 20 − 16	22. 16 − 13	23. 18 − 14	24. 12 − 12
25. 19 − 19	26. 20 − 19	27. 15 − 15	28. 18 − 16	29. 13 − 12	30. 17 − 16
31. 20 − 11	32. 16 − 11	33. 18 − 17	34. 19 − 14	35. 13 − 10	36. 13 − 11
37. 17 − 11	38. 13 − 13	39. 14 − 10	40. 12 − 11	41. 18 − 18	42. 14 − 12
43. 10 − 10	44. 19 − 12	45. 20 − 14	46. 20 − 10	47. 18 − 15	48. 16 − 16
49. 19 − 10	50. 15 − 10	51. 20 − 15	52. 20 − 20	53. 17 − 12	54. 16 − 12
55. 11 − 10	56. 18 − 10	57. 17 − 10	58. 17 − 13	59. 20 − 13	60. 17 − 17

1. 19 − 14	2. 17 − 17	3. 17 − 16	4. 11 − 11	5. 16 − 11	6. 14 − 14
7. 18 − 17	8. 19 − 17	9. 18 − 15	10. 11 − 10	11. 17 − 11	12. 19 − 10
13. 20 − 14	14. 18 − 12	15. 18 − 13	16. 16 − 14	17. 13 − 11	18. 10 − 10
19. 17 − 14	20. 20 − 20	21. 13 − 13	22. 17 − 15	23. 12 − 12	24. 19 − 13
25. 18 − 11	26. 20 − 17	27. 16 − 13	28. 19 − 19	29. 18 − 18	30. 19 − 16
31. 15 − 15	32. 15 − 12	33. 17 − 10	34. 18 − 14	35. 13 − 12	36. 12 − 11
37. 15 − 13	38. 14 − 11	39. 16 − 10	40. 20 − 19	41. 20 − 11	42. 19 − 11
43. 20 − 18	44. 19 − 18	45. 15 − 11	46. 14 − 12	47. 16 − 16	48. 16 − 15
49. 20 − 13	50. 18 − 16	51. 19 − 12	52. 17 − 12	53. 20 − 15	54. 13 − 10
55. 14 − 13	56. 15 − 14	57. 12 − 10	58. 17 − 13	59. 19 − 15	60. 15 − 10

1. $\begin{array}{r}7\\-\ 7\\\hline\end{array}$	2. $\begin{array}{r}15\\-\ 15\\\hline\end{array}$	3. $\begin{array}{r}9\\-\ 9\\\hline\end{array}$	4. $\begin{array}{r}18\\-\ 3\\\hline\end{array}$	5. $\begin{array}{r}14\\-\ 4\\\hline\end{array}$	6. $\begin{array}{r}17\\-\ 17\\\hline\end{array}$
7. $\begin{array}{r}17\\-\ 13\\\hline\end{array}$	8. $\begin{array}{r}18\\-\ 1\\\hline\end{array}$	9. $\begin{array}{r}18\\-\ 5\\\hline\end{array}$	10. $\begin{array}{r}9\\-\ 1\\\hline\end{array}$	11. $\begin{array}{r}10\\-\ 9\\\hline\end{array}$	12. $\begin{array}{r}14\\-\ 0\\\hline\end{array}$
13. $\begin{array}{r}16\\-\ 8\\\hline\end{array}$	14. $\begin{array}{r}18\\-\ 8\\\hline\end{array}$	15. $\begin{array}{r}18\\-\ 17\\\hline\end{array}$	16. $\begin{array}{r}1\\-\ 1\\\hline\end{array}$	17. $\begin{array}{r}16\\-\ 5\\\hline\end{array}$	18. $\begin{array}{r}9\\-\ 8\\\hline\end{array}$
19. $\begin{array}{r}16\\-\ 10\\\hline\end{array}$	20. $\begin{array}{r}15\\-\ 8\\\hline\end{array}$	21. $\begin{array}{r}12\\-\ 1\\\hline\end{array}$	22. $\begin{array}{r}9\\-\ 4\\\hline\end{array}$	23. $\begin{array}{r}13\\-\ 0\\\hline\end{array}$	24. $\begin{array}{r}17\\-\ 4\\\hline\end{array}$
25. $\begin{array}{r}20\\-\ 8\\\hline\end{array}$	26. $\begin{array}{r}18\\-\ 2\\\hline\end{array}$	27. $\begin{array}{r}8\\-\ 2\\\hline\end{array}$	28. $\begin{array}{r}8\\-\ 1\\\hline\end{array}$	29. $\begin{array}{r}17\\-\ 1\\\hline\end{array}$	30. $\begin{array}{r}9\\-\ 7\\\hline\end{array}$
31. $\begin{array}{r}15\\-\ 13\\\hline\end{array}$	32. $\begin{array}{r}15\\-\ 6\\\hline\end{array}$	33. $\begin{array}{r}19\\-\ 18\\\hline\end{array}$	34. $\begin{array}{r}7\\-\ 0\\\hline\end{array}$	35. $\begin{array}{r}20\\-\ 7\\\hline\end{array}$	36. $\begin{array}{r}8\\-\ 7\\\hline\end{array}$
37. $\begin{array}{r}16\\-\ 1\\\hline\end{array}$	38. $\begin{array}{r}11\\-\ 3\\\hline\end{array}$	39. $\begin{array}{r}18\\-\ 15\\\hline\end{array}$	40. $\begin{array}{r}4\\-\ 2\\\hline\end{array}$	41. $\begin{array}{r}20\\-\ 11\\\hline\end{array}$	42. $\begin{array}{r}4\\-\ 3\\\hline\end{array}$
43. $\begin{array}{r}12\\-\ 0\\\hline\end{array}$	44. $\begin{array}{r}10\\-\ 2\\\hline\end{array}$	45. $\begin{array}{r}10\\-\ 5\\\hline\end{array}$	46. $\begin{array}{r}11\\-\ 8\\\hline\end{array}$	47. $\begin{array}{r}11\\-\ 11\\\hline\end{array}$	48. $\begin{array}{r}20\\-\ 17\\\hline\end{array}$
49. $\begin{array}{r}12\\-\ 11\\\hline\end{array}$	50. $\begin{array}{r}18\\-\ 18\\\hline\end{array}$	51. $\begin{array}{r}16\\-\ 3\\\hline\end{array}$	52. $\begin{array}{r}16\\-\ 11\\\hline\end{array}$	53. $\begin{array}{r}11\\-\ 1\\\hline\end{array}$	54. $\begin{array}{r}11\\-\ 10\\\hline\end{array}$
55. $\begin{array}{r}16\\-\ 14\\\hline\end{array}$	56. $\begin{array}{r}15\\-\ 4\\\hline\end{array}$	57. $\begin{array}{r}5\\-\ 1\\\hline\end{array}$	58. $\begin{array}{r}17\\-\ 0\\\hline\end{array}$	59. $\begin{array}{r}9\\-\ 5\\\hline\end{array}$	60. $\begin{array}{r}14\\-\ 14\\\hline\end{array}$

1. 4 − 2	2. 15 − 12	3. 20 − 19	4. 13 − 4	5. 8 − 5	6. 11 − 10
7. 10 − 2	8. 13 − 2	9. 3 − 1	10. 18 − 7	11. 16 − 15	12. 14 − 7
13. 18 − 18	14. 3 − 2	15. 2 − 2	16. 1 − 0	17. 9 − 1	18. 17 − 12
19. 7 − 1	20. 13 − 10	21. 11 − 5	22. 18 − 9	23. 10 − 0	24. 15 − 3
25. 16 − 6	26. 18 − 15	27. 18 − 6	28. 16 − 5	29. 19 − 12	30. 20 − 10
31. 13 − 5	32. 19 − 19	33. 11 − 7	34. 15 − 13	35. 3 − 0	36. 19 − 10
37. 10 − 9	38. 18 − 3	39. 19 − 1	40. 2 − 0	41. 16 − 16	42. 10 − 4
43. 17 − 7	44. 8 − 6	45. 20 − 11	46. 7 − 7	47. 14 − 13	48. 13 − 7
49. 19 − 17	50. 8 − 4	51. 14 − 6	52. 20 − 15	53. 13 − 13	54. 12 − 6
55. 20 − 9	56. 5 − 0	57. 15 − 9	58. 12 − 4	59. 16 − 9	60. 7 − 4

1.   6
  - 4
	2. 13
	  - 13
		3. 18
		  - 12
			4. 11
			  - 11
				5. 11
				  - 5
					6. 19
					  - 5

7.   19
  - 1
	8. 11
	  - 4
		9. 16
		  - 12
			10. 3
			  - 1
				11. 14
				  - 3
					12. 15
					  - 13

13.   17
  - 11
	14. 15
	  - 15
		15. 13
		  - 9
			16. 16
			  - 4
				17. 19
				  - 2
					18. 19
					  - 9

19.   8
  - 5
	20. 19
	  - 12
		21. 20
		  - 11
			22. 18
			  - 13
				23. 18
				  - 2
					24. 2
					  - 2

25.   15
  - 5
	26. 5
	  - 4
		27. 8
		  - 3
			28. 20
			  - 8
				29. 18
				  - 15
					30. 11
					  - 3

31.   19
  - 4
	32. 7
	  - 5
		33. 18
		  - 10
			34. 17
			  - 15
				35. 12
				  - 2
					36. 7
					  - 7

37.   2
  - 1
	38. 20
	  - 13
		39. 16
		  - 6
			40. 14
			  - 8
				41. 6
				  - 0
					42. 19
					  - 3

43.   10
  - 5
	44. 15
	  - 4
		45. 3
		  - 2
			46. 14
			  - 12
				47. 14
				  - 11
					48. 18
					  - 18

49.   17
  - 3
	50. 19
	  - 18
		51. 14
		  - 5
			52. 18
			  - 14
				53. 19
				  - 8
					54. 14
					  - 2

55.   16
  - 0
	56. 18
	  - 16
		57. 12
		  - 3
			58. 20
			  - 15
				59. 14
				  - 13
					60. 16
					  - 3

1. 18 − 1	2. 17 − 11	3. 8 − 3	4. 12 − 10	5. 14 − 0	6. 11 − 7
7. 13 − 9	8. 12 − 4	9. 3 − 0	10. 20 − 2	11. 14 − 1	12. 19 − 10
13. 8 − 0	14. 10 − 6	15. 7 − 6	16. 19 − 2	17. 14 − 10	18. 15 − 3
19. 18 − 17	20. 11 − 6	21. 10 − 7	22. 16 − 14	23. 19 − 12	24. 19 − 6
25. 8 − 1	26. 15 − 5	27. 19 − 11	28. 9 − 4	29. 16 − 5	30. 13 − 5
31. 3 − 2	32. 5 − 3	33. 18 − 15	34. 14 − 7	35. 14 − 13	36. 14 − 14
37. 20 − 11	38. 15 − 14	39. 19 − 16	40. 16 − 15	41. 15 − 10	42. 18 − 4
43. 14 − 8	44. 17 − 4	45. 2 − 0	46. 5 − 5	47. 18 − 18	48. 16 − 11
49. 12 − 5	50. 7 − 3	51. 19 − 19	52. 6 − 4	53. 9 − 1	54. 7 − 1
55. 16 − 1	56. 10 − 1	57. 14 − 2	58. 7 − 2	59. 6 − 2	60. 13 − 11

1.   5
  - 1
	2. 15
	  - 15
		3. 15
		  - 14
			4. 3
			  - 1
				5. 18
				  - 7
					6. 6
					  - 6

7.   18
  - 15
	8. 20
	  - 16
		9. 8
		  - 2
			10. 18
			  - 3
				11. 19
				  - 3
					12. 10
					  - 5

13.   17
  - 11
	14. 5
	  - 5
		15. 14
		  - 5
			16. 12
			  - 7
				17. 13
				  - 6
					18. 19
					  - 8

19.   17
  - 15
	20. 20
	  - 6
		21. 15
		  - 13
			22. 19
			  - 7
				23. 17
				  - 16
					24. 19
					  - 9

25.   13
  - 4
	26. 11
	  - 10
		27. 17
		  - 10
			28. 14
			  - 13
				29. 18
				  - 9
					30. 18
					  - 10

31.   20
  - 1
	32. 13
	  - 1
		33. 16
		  - 9
			34. 7
			  - 2
				35. 19
				  - 16
					36. 6
					  - 5

37.   7
  - 1
	38. 13
	  - 3
		39. 11
		  - 6
			40. 19
			  - 13
				41. 9
				  - 3
					42. 19
					  - 19

43.   4
  - 0
	44. 4
	  - 4
		45. 18
		  - 12
			46. 17
			  - 2
				47. 13
				  - 2
					48. 18
					  - 14

49.   17
  - 3
	50. 14
	  - 7
		51. 20
		  - 13
			52. 9
			  - 7
				53. 8
				  - 7
					54. 17
					  - 9

55.   4
  - 1
	56. 16
	  - 0
		57. 17
		  - 5
			58. 9
			  - 9
				59. 17
				  - 0
					60. 13
					  - 11

1. 12 − 6	2. 6 − 1	3. 14 − 10	4. 6 − 2	5. 3 − 1	6. 8 − 1
7. 19 − 14	8. 5 − 0	9. 13 − 11	10. 7 − 2	11. 1 − 0	12. 19 − 3
13. 16 − 16	14. 18 − 2	15. 16 − 2	16. 18 − 15	17. 13 − 0	18. 10 − 7
19. 16 − 9	20. 9 − 6	21. 12 − 4	22. 13 − 4	23. 14 − 6	24. 5 − 3
25. 15 − 3	26. 13 − 12	27. 8 − 3	28. 10 − 4	29. 6 − 4	30. 9 − 5
31. 19 − 10	32. 13 − 10	33. 15 − 6	34. 18 − 7	35. 2 − 2	36. 18 − 5
37. 15 − 13	38. 16 − 5	39. 8 − 4	40. 12 − 7	41. 16 − 1	42. 17 − 12
43. 11 − 8	44. 7 − 7	45. 20 − 13	46. 17 − 7	47. 14 − 2	48. 12 − 3
49. 14 − 1	50. 19 − 6	51. 18 − 0	52. 14 − 0	53. 20 − 17	54. 17 − 15
55. 10 − 2	56. 19 − 15	57. 17 − 8	58. 18 − 18	59. 15 − 7	60. 18 − 17

1. 9 − 9	2. 12 − 2	3. 1 − 0	4. 17 − 5	5. 12 − 1	6. 18 − 2
7. 10 − 8	8. 4 − 3	9. 11 − 6	10. 15 − 1	11. 13 − 7	12. 11 − 0
13. 12 − 12	14. 13 − 9	15. 18 − 6	16. 15 − 3	17. 18 − 11	18. 5 − 3
19. 19 − 13	20. 16 − 2	21. 6 − 0	22. 14 − 8	23. 19 − 1	24. 8 − 8
25. 3 − 2	26. 17 − 16	27. 19 − 14	28. 12 − 5	29. 15 − 13	30. 5 − 1
31. 17 − 4	32. 13 − 1	33. 8 − 5	34. 18 − 9	35. 20 − 6	36. 4 − 1
37. 17 − 0	38. 13 − 11	39. 6 − 6	40. 7 − 6	41. 14 − 4	42. 20 − 9
43. 20 − 15	44. 10 − 1	45. 18 − 5	46. 19 − 18	47. 20 − 13	48. 3 − 0
49. 3 − 1	50. 12 − 9	51. 15 − 9	52. 7 − 4	53. 15 − 4	54. 14 − 11
55. 8 − 2	56. 14 − 9	57. 6 − 1	58. 16 − 4	59. 17 − 15	60. 12 − 10

1. $16 - 15$	2. $14 - 4$	3. $12 - 5$	4. $12 - 4$	5. $7 - 5$	6. $0 - 0$
7. $14 - 7$	8. $8 - 1$	9. $12 - 8$	10. $18 - 11$	11. $16 - 3$	12. $16 - 14$
13. $18 - 6$	14. $17 - 17$	15. $15 - 5$	16. $12 - 3$	17. $19 - 19$	18. $15 - 8$
19. $5 - 2$	20. $10 - 7$	21. $19 - 7$	22. $18 - 2$	23. $12 - 0$	24. $12 - 9$
25. $18 - 10$	26. $5 - 3$	27. $18 - 17$	28. $19 - 9$	29. $8 - 6$	30. $12 - 10$
31. $19 - 12$	32. $9 - 5$	33. $9 - 9$	34. $17 - 4$	35. $20 - 16$	36. $18 - 8$
37. $8 - 2$	38. $19 - 5$	39. $11 - 1$	40. $15 - 2$	41. $13 - 11$	42. $13 - 8$
43. $9 - 3$	44. $17 - 12$	45. $19 - 1$	46. $6 - 4$	47. $10 - 6$	48. $19 - 2$
49. $20 - 18$	50. $18 - 14$	51. $19 - 4$	52. $18 - 4$	53. $10 - 0$	54. $13 - 6$
55. $18 - 1$	56. $6 - 3$	57. $10 - 3$	58. $14 - 3$	59. $16 - 2$	60. $4 - 3$

1. 12 − 5	2. 16 − 2	3. 15 − 4	4. 17 − 5	5. 3 − 0	6. 15 − 5
7. 17 − 2	8. 13 − 7	9. 20 − 3	10. 12 − 10	11. 20 − 19	12. 16 − 4
13. 7 − 7	14. 14 − 8	15. 14 − 3	16. 13 − 3	17. 19 − 12	18. 19 − 16
19. 18 − 7	20. 18 − 0	21. 17 − 1	22. 19 − 9	23. 19 − 14	24. 16 − 16
25. 15 − 15	26. 16 − 5	27. 1 − 1	28. 9 − 9	29. 16 − 12	30. 9 − 7
31. 17 − 14	32. 20 − 4	33. 12 − 4	34. 10 − 2	35. 18 − 16	36. 19 − 1
37. 15 − 9	38. 6 − 5	39. 20 − 6	40. 10 − 9	41. 13 − 5	42. 7 − 6
43. 10 − 4	44. 16 − 1	45. 6 − 0	46. 5 − 0	47. 12 − 3	48. 15 − 6
49. 20 − 15	50. 20 − 7	51. 18 − 4	52. 5 − 4	53. 13 − 4	54. 9 − 1
55. 19 − 2	56. 17 − 8	57. 9 − 5	58. 14 − 2	59. 6 − 1	60. 17 − 12

1.   18
   - 11
	2. 14
	   - 14
		3. 10
		   - 10
			4. 16
			   - 16
				5. 19
				   - 10
					6. 10
					   - 5

7.   18
   - 8
	8. 7
	   - 2
		9. 6
		   - 4
			10. 4
			   - 0
				11. 9
				   - 1
					12. 8
					   - 6

13.   10
   - 8
	14. 14
	   - 3
		15. 4
		   - 2
			16. 16
			   - 2
				17. 6
				   - 5
					18. 6
					   - 3

19.   2
   - 0
	20. 7
	   - 3
		21. 19
		   - 16
			22. 20
			   - 4
				23. 8
				   - 2
					24. 10
					   - 4

25.   19
   - 19
	26. 10
	   - 2
		27. 18
		   - 0
			28. 12
			   - 1
				29. 16
				   - 7
					30. 13
					   - 0

31.   20
   - 14
	32. 13
	   - 4
		33. 19
		   - 12
			34. 15
			   - 8
				35. 12
				   - 11
					36. 19
					   - 5

37.   15
   - 9
	38. 3
	   - 1
		39. 18
		   - 16
			40. 18
			   - 1
				41. 19
				   - 14
					42. 18
					   - 3

43.   12
   - 8
	44. 15
	   - 2
		45. 20
		   - 15
			46. 9
			   - 9
				47. 16
				   - 3
					48. 15
					   - 4

49.   14
   - 2
	50. 10
	   - 1
		51. 11
		   - 9
			52. 12
			   - 3
				53. 11
				   - 5
					54. 16
					   - 1

55.   16
   - 10
	56. 15
	   - 12
		57. 14
		   - 13
			58. 13
			   - 1
				59. 16
				   - 4
					60. 18
					   - 4

1. 20 − 7	2. 17 − 12	3. 16 − 2	4. 19 − 10	5. 5 − 1	6. 15 − 5
7. 17 − 1	8. 17 − 5	9. 19 − 5	10. 16 − 13	11. 14 − 10	12. 13 − 10
13. 14 − 8	14. 8 − 6	15. 16 − 1	16. 14 − 4	17. 17 − 9	18. 15 − 2
19. 18 − 14	20. 9 − 4	21. 17 − 7	22. 13 − 7	23. 16 − 10	24. 17 − 11
25. 20 − 14	26. 14 − 11	27. 13 − 5	28. 17 − 14	29. 16 − 4	30. 16 − 14
31. 17 − 17	32. 16 − 15	33. 10 − 6	34. 14 − 3	35. 8 − 8	36. 14 − 13
37. 9 − 9	38. 12 − 9	39. 17 − 3	40. 18 − 6	41. 12 − 6	42. 9 − 0
43. 8 − 2	44. 6 − 1	45. 9 − 1	46. 4 − 1	47. 14 − 1	48. 12 − 4
49. 18 − 18	50. 15 − 14	51. 11 − 3	52. 20 − 8	53. 15 − 1	54. 16 − 0
55. 20 − 13	56. 17 − 15	57. 6 − 5	58. 10 − 1	59. 14 − 14	60. 16 − 16

1. 18 − 3	2. 18 − 12	3. 11 − 10
4. 10 − 0	5. 14 − 13	6. 19 − 8
7. 15 − 7	8. 11 − 3	9. 18 − 6
10. 19 − 7	11. 1 − 1	12. 13 − 10
13. 20 − 8	14. 13 − 7	15. 7 − 5
16. 18 − 8	17. 17 − 4	18. 8 − 6
19. 16 − 4	20. 14 − 4	21. 19 − 3
22. 15 − 6	23. 19 − 14	24. 9 − 0
25. 20 − 15	26. 10 − 5	27. 10 − 9
28. 17 − 17	29. 18 − 5	30. 19 − 0
31. 12 − 11	32. 19 − 1	33. 13 − 3
34. 14 − 2	35. 4 − 3	36. 10 − 3
37. 15 − 11	38. 19 − 5	39. 14 − 0
40. 18 − 18	41. 9 − 9	42. 15 − 12
43. 16 − 6	44. 20 − 0	45. 8 − 5
46. 9 − 6	47. 15 − 5	48. 16 − 15
49. 16 − 12	50. 19 − 9	51. 2 − 0
52. 13 − 6	53. 20 − 6	54. 7 − 6
55. 6 − 6	56. 15 − 0	57. 9 − 3
58. 10 − 6	59. 17 − 15	60. 18 − 2

Day 63

Subtracting Digits 0 - 20

NAME:___________   TIME: Score: /60

1.   14
  - 9
	2. 4
	  - 0
		3. 13
		  - 6
			4. 14
			  - 7
				5. 12
				  - 8
					6. 17
					  - 16

7.   18
  - 8
	8. 10
	  - 2
		9. 14
		  - 8
			10. 7
			  - 5
				11. 20
				  - 2
					12. 8
					  - 3

13.   17
  - 9
	14. 20
	  - 18
		15. 17
		  - 15
			16. 19
			  - 5
				17. 17
				  - 2
					18. 8
					  - 8

19.   15
  - 11
	20. 15
	  - 9
		21. 12
		  - 12
			22. 8
			  - 4
				23. 13
				  - 2
					24. 15
					  - 5

25.   8
  - 1
	26. 14
	  - 5
		27. 19
		  - 0
			28. 16
			  - 14
				29. 16
				  - 3
					30. 5
					  - 4

31.   16
  - 9
	32. 17
	  - 6
		33. 10
		  - 0
			34. 13
			  - 0
				35. 13
				  - 1
					36. 9
					  - 1

37.   13
  - 8
	38. 17
	  - 3
		39. 17
		  - 1
			40. 16
			  - 2
				41. 13
				  - 11
					42. 18
					  - 16

43.   11
  - 8
	44. 9
	  - 6
		45. 16
		  - 1
			46. 18
			  - 2
				47. 14
				  - 3
					48. 2
					  - 1

49.   11
  - 3
	50. 9
	  - 3
		51. 10
		  - 7
			52. 15
			  - 8
				53. 7
				  - 7
					54. 14
					  - 4

55.   2
  - 2
	56. 17
	  - 8
		57. 18
		  - 12
			58. 20
			  - 19
				59. 12
				  - 7
					60. 15
					  - 7

Day 64
Subtracting Digits 0 - 20

1. 13 − 7	2. 19 − 15	3. 15 − 4	4. 20 − 4	5. 16 − 7	6. 16 − 5
7. 20 − 18	8. 16 − 13	9. 5 − 1	10. 14 − 6	11. 12 − 12	12. 6 − 4
13. 20 − 9	14. 5 − 2	15. 17 − 16	16. 19 − 4	17. 17 − 9	18. 18 − 7
19. 9 − 9	20. 20 − 0	21. 4 − 1	22. 17 − 8	23. 18 − 9	24. 15 − 10
25. 14 − 11	26. 10 − 3	27. 20 − 16	28. 14 − 10	29. 5 − 0	30. 12 − 9
31. 18 − 18	32. 19 − 5	33. 14 − 13	34. 15 − 5	35. 17 − 15	36. 8 − 5
37. 12 − 10	38. 11 − 10	39. 18 − 8	40. 19 − 17	41. 16 − 10	42. 11 − 2
43. 13 − 10	44. 18 − 15	45. 10 − 2	46. 3 − 1	47. 18 − 11	48. 4 − 3
49. 19 − 18	50. 5 − 4	51. 12 − 6	52. 17 − 5	53. 17 − 2	54. 14 − 0
55. 7 − 3	56. 17 − 17	57. 20 − 20	58. 10 − 4	59. 17 − 3	60. 15 − 14

Day 65

Subtracting Digits 0 - 20

NAME: ___________   TIME: ___________   Score: /60

1. $\begin{array}{r}11\\-10\\\hline\end{array}$	2. $\begin{array}{r}19\\-13\\\hline\end{array}$	3. $\begin{array}{r}17\\-2\\\hline\end{array}$	4. $\begin{array}{r}14\\-3\\\hline\end{array}$	5. $\begin{array}{r}14\\-6\\\hline\end{array}$	6. $\begin{array}{r}8\\-7\\\hline\end{array}$
7. $\begin{array}{r}4\\-4\\\hline\end{array}$	8. $\begin{array}{r}16\\-2\\\hline\end{array}$	9. $\begin{array}{r}17\\-14\\\hline\end{array}$	10. $\begin{array}{r}10\\-6\\\hline\end{array}$	11. $\begin{array}{r}11\\-11\\\hline\end{array}$	12. $\begin{array}{r}9\\-7\\\hline\end{array}$
13. $\begin{array}{r}18\\-16\\\hline\end{array}$	14. $\begin{array}{r}20\\-5\\\hline\end{array}$	15. $\begin{array}{r}17\\-17\\\hline\end{array}$	16. $\begin{array}{r}20\\-11\\\hline\end{array}$	17. $\begin{array}{r}16\\-3\\\hline\end{array}$	18. $\begin{array}{r}15\\-6\\\hline\end{array}$
19. $\begin{array}{r}13\\-10\\\hline\end{array}$	20. $\begin{array}{r}14\\-4\\\hline\end{array}$	21. $\begin{array}{r}19\\-8\\\hline\end{array}$	22. $\begin{array}{r}14\\-14\\\hline\end{array}$	23. $\begin{array}{r}16\\-12\\\hline\end{array}$	24. $\begin{array}{r}14\\-1\\\hline\end{array}$
25. $\begin{array}{r}11\\-3\\\hline\end{array}$	26. $\begin{array}{r}15\\-8\\\hline\end{array}$	27. $\begin{array}{r}13\\-3\\\hline\end{array}$	28. $\begin{array}{r}18\\-0\\\hline\end{array}$	29. $\begin{array}{r}12\\-4\\\hline\end{array}$	30. $\begin{array}{r}16\\-7\\\hline\end{array}$
31. $\begin{array}{r}19\\-1\\\hline\end{array}$	32. $\begin{array}{r}13\\-2\\\hline\end{array}$	33. $\begin{array}{r}13\\-6\\\hline\end{array}$	34. $\begin{array}{r}18\\-7\\\hline\end{array}$	35. $\begin{array}{r}13\\-8\\\hline\end{array}$	36. $\begin{array}{r}18\\-5\\\hline\end{array}$
37. $\begin{array}{r}18\\-2\\\hline\end{array}$	38. $\begin{array}{r}12\\-8\\\hline\end{array}$	39. $\begin{array}{r}18\\-12\\\hline\end{array}$	40. $\begin{array}{r}18\\-6\\\hline\end{array}$	41. $\begin{array}{r}3\\-3\\\hline\end{array}$	42. $\begin{array}{r}8\\-8\\\hline\end{array}$
43. $\begin{array}{r}15\\-14\\\hline\end{array}$	44. $\begin{array}{r}14\\-2\\\hline\end{array}$	45. $\begin{array}{r}10\\-4\\\hline\end{array}$	46. $\begin{array}{r}19\\-18\\\hline\end{array}$	47. $\begin{array}{r}14\\-5\\\hline\end{array}$	48. $\begin{array}{r}4\\-2\\\hline\end{array}$
49. $\begin{array}{r}19\\-5\\\hline\end{array}$	50. $\begin{array}{r}9\\-3\\\hline\end{array}$	51. $\begin{array}{r}18\\-11\\\hline\end{array}$	52. $\begin{array}{r}2\\-2\\\hline\end{array}$	53. $\begin{array}{r}20\\-13\\\hline\end{array}$	54. $\begin{array}{r}16\\-5\\\hline\end{array}$
55. $\begin{array}{r}13\\-4\\\hline\end{array}$	56. $\begin{array}{r}18\\-13\\\hline\end{array}$	57. $\begin{array}{r}17\\-5\\\hline\end{array}$	58. $\begin{array}{r}19\\-6\\\hline\end{array}$	59. $\begin{array}{r}9\\-2\\\hline\end{array}$	60. $\begin{array}{r}6\\-6\\\hline\end{array}$

1. 9 − 7	2. 16 − 7	3. 7 − 1
4. 17 − 3	5. 10 − 10	6. 17 − 16
7. 11 − 6	8. 1 − 1	9. 18 − 9
10. 18 − 12	11. 20 − 1	12. 15 − 1
13. 7 − 7	14. 8 − 2	15. 10 − 2
16. 9 − 0	17. 9 − 4	18. 8 − 6
19. 12 − 1	20. 11 − 11	21. 12 − 2
22. 18 − 1	23. 15 − 7	24. 7 − 3
25. 15 − 12	26. 14 − 4	27. 13 − 12
28. 14 − 10	29. 16 − 10	30. 20 − 17
31. 16 − 1	32. 18 − 11	33. 19 − 19
34. 3 − 0	35. 5 − 0	36. 5 − 5
37. 8 − 8	38. 9 − 6	39. 19 − 15
40. 12 − 9	41. 16 − 8	42. 10 − 4
43. 2 − 1	44. 16 − 11	45. 18 − 13
46. 17 − 1	47. 14 − 3	48. 17 − 12
49. 19 − 3	50. 18 − 10	51. 18 − 2
52. 17 − 9	53. 19 − 12	54. 6 − 3
55. 13 − 9	56. 17 − 11	57. 17 − 13
58. 20 − 16	59. 15 − 2	60. 18 − 6

1. 5 − 3	2. 19 − 5	3. 14 − 7	4. 16 − 6	5. 10 − 10	6. 12 − 9
7. 14 − 6	8. 14 − 13	9. 12 − 6	10. 11 − 0	11. 15 − 11	12. 19 − 2
13. 8 − 8	14. 13 − 5	15. 9 − 7	16. 18 − 1	17. 20 − 9	18. 12 − 7
19. 11 − 7	20. 16 − 16	21. 18 − 4	22. 18 − 14	23. 14 − 14	24. 12 − 10
25. 10 − 2	26. 4 − 1	27. 18 − 18	28. 16 − 4	29. 17 − 10	30. 8 − 7
31. 9 − 4	32. 2 − 1	33. 17 − 14	34. 7 − 1	35. 18 − 12	36. 11 − 5
37. 14 − 8	38. 13 − 1	39. 11 − 2	40. 17 − 16	41. 15 − 14	42. 17 − 4
43. 12 − 4	44. 19 − 6	45. 13 − 7	46. 15 − 0	47. 15 − 9	48. 17 − 11
49. 4 − 4	50. 8 − 2	51. 20 − 18	52. 15 − 7	53. 19 − 11	54. 17 − 1
55. 19 − 18	56. 12 − 12	57. 15 − 10	58. 14 − 12	59. 13 − 3	60. 20 − 6

1.   8
  − 5
	2. 14
	  − 3
		3. 8
		  − 6
			4. 16
			  − 16
				5. 13
				  − 4
					6. 15
					  − 14

7.   17
  − 15
	8. 17
	  − 12
		9. 13
		  − 9
			10. 17
			  − 1
				11. 7
				  − 6
					12. 1
					  − 0

13.   19
  − 16
	14. 20
	  − 3
		15. 12
		  − 5
			16. 17
			  − 14
				17. 9
				  − 9
					18. 13
					  − 7

19.   7
  − 3
	20. 19
	  − 9
		21. 8
		  − 0
			22. 8
			  − 2
				23. 18
				  − 14
					24. 14
					  − 5

25.   12
  − 11
	26. 15
	  − 9
		27. 12
		  − 4
			28. 16
			  − 9
				29. 6
				  − 2
					30. 4
					  − 1

31.   11
  − 0
	32. 15
	  − 5
		33. 2
		  − 1
			34. 6
			  − 0
				35. 18
				  − 17
					36. 18
					  − 11

37.   17
  − 5
	38. 16
	  − 10
		39. 19
		  − 6
			40. 17
			  − 11
				41. 14
				  − 6
					42. 16
					  − 11

43.   15
  − 2
	44. 9
	  − 2
		45. 13
		  − 3
			46. 11
			  − 2
				47. 15
				  − 10
					48. 8
					  − 8

49.   14
  − 13
	50. 16
	  − 13
		51. 16
		  − 12
			52. 17
			  − 3
				53. 16
				  − 6
					54. 19
					  − 13

55.   7
  − 7
	56. 13
	  − 2
		57. 16
		  − 1
			58. 15
			  − 13
				59. 19
				  − 15
					60. 15
					  − 4

1. 19 − 14	2. 16 − 1	3. 8 − 0	4. 8 − 4	5. 16 − 11	6. 16 − 0
7. 17 − 9	8. 18 − 10	9. 15 − 8	10. 10 − 7	11. 13 − 5	12. 15 − 6
13. 14 − 7	14. 9 − 4	15. 14 − 4	16. 10 − 6	17. 17 − 10	18. 16 − 6
19. 7 − 0	20. 10 − 1	21. 11 − 11	22. 6 − 4	23. 10 − 2	24. 12 − 8
25. 8 − 1	26. 18 − 7	27. 9 − 6	28. 19 − 1	29. 17 − 3	30. 19 − 8
31. 18 − 9	32. 9 − 1	33. 16 − 7	34. 16 − 12	35. 14 − 1	36. 10 − 5
37. 7 − 1	38. 8 − 7	39. 18 − 13	40. 16 − 15	41. 11 − 8	42. 17 − 8
43. 19 − 16	44. 15 − 13	45. 17 − 11	46. 19 − 6	47. 11 − 4	48. 8 − 3
49. 7 − 3	50. 16 − 10	51. 12 − 1	52. 14 − 12	53. 12 − 5	54. 16 − 4
55. 17 − 17	56. 17 − 7	57. 19 − 4	58. 10 − 8	59. 11 − 3	60. 18 − 4

1. 7 − 7	2. 15 − 9	3. 15 − 6	4. 4 − 3	5. 9 − 1	6. 8 − 3
7. 19 − 12	8. 9 − 7	9. 16 − 4	10. 11 − 4	11. 6 − 5	12. 10 − 0
13. 17 − 4	14. 7 − 6	15. 14 − 11	16. 17 − 12	17. 20 − 18	18. 9 − 9
19. 8 − 1	20. 7 − 5	21. 3 − 3	22. 19 − 3	23. 18 − 12	24. 6 − 4
25. 8 − 4	26. 18 − 18	27. 16 − 12	28. 19 − 9	29. 18 − 6	30. 15 − 0
31. 19 − 15	32. 15 − 8	33. 12 − 9	34. 20 − 14	35. 19 − 17	36. 8 − 6
37. 15 − 1	38. 20 − 17	39. 9 − 3	40. 15 − 2	41. 4 − 2	42. 11 − 3
43. 10 − 1	44. 9 − 5	45. 12 − 4	46. 12 − 3	47. 14 − 6	48. 8 − 8
49. 5 − 3	50. 15 − 7	51. 18 − 17	52. 14 − 14	53. 17 − 3	54. 8 − 0
55. 18 − 3	56. 16 − 14	57. 5 − 4	58. 4 − 4	59. 1 − 0	60. 16 − 10

Day 71
Subtracting Digits 0 - 20

NAME: ___________   TIME: Score: /60

1. 20 − 16	2. 8 − 6	3. 12 − 11	4. 18 − 18	5. 18 − 14	6. 18 − 15
7. 17 − 1	8. 18 − 10	9. 9 − 1	10. 5 − 3	11. 4 − 1	12. 19 − 2
13. 14 − 0	14. 16 − 3	15. 14 − 2	16. 7 − 5	17. 19 − 10	18. 19 − 16
19. 12 − 7	20. 10 − 8	21. 8 − 1	22. 5 − 1	23. 19 − 4	24. 19 − 3
25. 17 − 8	26. 11 − 8	27. 17 − 2	28. 16 − 1	29. 15 − 13	30. 14 − 4
31. 17 − 9	32. 9 − 8	33. 13 − 8	34. 17 − 15	35. 11 − 2	36. 17 − 12
37. 17 − 13	38. 9 − 7	39. 13 − 1	40. 11 − 0	41. 19 − 9	42. 9 − 2
43. 20 − 2	44. 19 − 1	45. 19 − 12	46. 14 − 8	47. 12 − 3	48. 3 − 2
49. 11 − 1	50. 19 − 15	51. 10 − 2	52. 18 − 9	53. 6 − 3	54. 7 − 7
55. 13 − 9	56. 20 − 5	57. 17 − 7	58. 15 − 3	59. 13 − 13	60. 9 − 6

Day 72
Subtracting Digits 0 - 20

NAME: ___________   TIME: Score: /60

1. 15 − 10	2. 15 − 6	3. 19 − 14	4. 14 − 8	5. 5 − 2	6. 16 − 3
7. 17 − 6	8. 19 − 15	9. 17 − 17	10. 16 − 15	11. 13 − 1	12. 19 − 16
13. 10 − 9	14. 20 − 16	15. 11 − 4	16. 19 − 11	17. 1 − 0	18. 17 − 11
19. 6 − 2	20. 10 − 2	21. 10 − 7	22. 13 − 5	23. 16 − 4	24. 17 − 16
25. 11 − 5	26. 6 − 6	27. 16 − 2	28. 18 − 12	29. 14 − 6	30. 19 − 0
31. 20 − 7	32. 12 − 11	33. 15 − 8	34. 18 − 18	35. 18 − 8	36. 17 − 5
37. 12 − 3	38. 19 − 8	39. 12 − 1	40. 9 − 7	41. 19 − 2	42. 20 − 12
43. 11 − 0	44. 18 − 13	45. 15 − 11	46. 3 − 1	47. 19 − 17	48. 14 − 12
49. 19 − 10	50. 4 − 2	51. 16 − 14	52. 8 − 5	53. 5 − 3	54. 20 − 6
55. 19 − 9	56. 4 − 4	57. 12 − 12	58. 9 − 5	59. 7 − 1	60. 15 − 1

1. $16 - 3$	2. $15 - 3$	3. $18 - 3$	4. $2 - 0$	5. $16 - 4$	6. $11 - 3$
7. $16 - 13$	8. $8 - 6$	9. $7 - 7$	10. $14 - 13$	11. $15 - 2$	12. $18 - 4$
13. $12 - 12$	14. $4 - 1$	15. $15 - 13$	16. $19 - 4$	17. $11 - 9$	18. $9 - 2$
19. $19 - 16$	20. $5 - 2$	21. $16 - 12$	22. $4 - 4$	23. $19 - 11$	24. $3 - 0$
25. $14 - 6$	26. $13 - 12$	27. $19 - 18$	28. $13 - 1$	29. $15 - 5$	30. $17 - 5$
31. $20 - 7$	32. $8 - 1$	33. $2 - 2$	34. $14 - 0$	35. $16 - 10$	36. $5 - 0$
37. $18 - 2$	38. $10 - 2$	39. $7 - 5$	40. $10 - 6$	41. $12 - 5$	42. $20 - 8$
43. $16 - 2$	44. $17 - 8$	45. $17 - 9$	46. $1 - 1$	47. $15 - 7$	48. $14 - 14$
49. $20 - 11$	50. $7 - 1$	51. $9 - 9$	52. $18 - 9$	53. $19 - 13$	54. $15 - 14$
55. $9 - 5$	56. $16 - 6$	57. $19 - 3$	58. $14 - 7$	59. $9 - 1$	60. $9 - 4$

1. $17 - 7$	2. $7 - 5$	3. $7 - 4$	4. $11 - 7$	5. $16 - 1$	6. $3 - 2$
7. $17 - 8$	8. $9 - 2$	9. $17 - 4$	10. $18 - 11$	11. $20 - 1$	12. $18 - 10$
13. $17 - 13$	14. $11 - 11$	15. $20 - 20$	16. $10 - 3$	17. $18 - 8$	18. $13 - 8$
19. $10 - 6$	20. $9 - 8$	21. $18 - 17$	22. $18 - 5$	23. $11 - 0$	24. $15 - 2$
25. $5 - 1$	26. $14 - 9$	27. $9 - 1$	28. $18 - 18$	29. $15 - 11$	30. $14 - 5$
31. $10 - 9$	32. $18 - 3$	33. $5 - 2$	34. $19 - 18$	35. $17 - 17$	36. $14 - 8$
37. $18 - 0$	38. $4 - 4$	39. $9 - 0$	40. $10 - 2$	41. $12 - 2$	42. $16 - 12$
43. $16 - 16$	44. $19 - 13$	45. $3 - 1$	46. $16 - 10$	47. $7 - 7$	48. $15 - 5$
49. $19 - 2$	50. $15 - 4$	51. $16 - 0$	52. $8 - 0$	53. $12 - 8$	54. $16 - 9$
55. $16 - 15$	56. $13 - 13$	57. $5 - 0$	58. $19 - 16$	59. $16 - 14$	60. $15 - 14$

#		#		#		#		#		#	
1.	10 − 1	2.	19 − 6	3.	19 − 5	4.	17 − 1	5.	14 − 11	6.	13 − 13
7.	18 − 16	8.	19 − 7	9.	15 − 6	10.	16 − 3	11.	19 − 13	12.	19 − 10
13.	20 − 3	14.	20 − 16	15.	15 − 7	16.	14 − 7	17.	15 − 3	18.	17 − 5
19.	5 − 2	20.	18 − 8	21.	13 − 4	22.	14 − 10	23.	13 − 1	24.	12 − 3
25.	20 − 2	26.	16 − 1	27.	15 − 13	28.	16 − 14	29.	5 − 1	30.	1 − 1
31.	15 − 11	32.	7 − 6	33.	15 − 12	34.	4 − 4	35.	17 − 0	36.	12 − 12
37.	9 − 1	38.	13 − 6	39.	13 − 0	40.	4 − 0	41.	12 − 11	42.	14 − 3
43.	8 − 4	44.	10 − 6	45.	20 − 19	46.	20 − 11	47.	19 − 2	48.	8 − 3
49.	20 − 7	50.	17 − 7	51.	17 − 6	52.	3 − 2	53.	8 − 7	54.	17 − 8
55.	16 − 0	56.	16 − 7	57.	12 − 2	58.	20 − 14	59.	7 − 2	60.	12 − 7

Day 76
Adding and Subtracting

NAME: __________ TIME: __________ Score: /60

1. $7 + 8$	2. $8 - 7$	3. $9 + 9$	4. $9 - 9$	5. $7 + 7$	6. $10 - 8$
7. $10 - 7$	8. $7 - 7$	9. $7 + 9$	10. $8 + 9$	11. $9 - 8$	12. $10 + 8$
13. $8 - 8$	14. $10 - 9$	15. $9 + 8$	16. $8 + 8$	17. $9 - 7$	18. $10 + 9$
19. $8 + 7$	20. $10 - 10$	21. $9 + 10$	22. $10 - 10$	23. $8 - 7$	24. $10 + 10$
25. $8 + 10$	26. $9 - 9$	27. $10 + 7$	28. $9 - 7$	29. $7 + 10$	30. $8 - 7$
31. $9 + 7$	32. $8 + 9$	33. $7 - 7$	34. $10 - 9$	35. $10 - 8$	36. $9 - 8$
37. $9 - 9$	38. $10 + 8$	39. $9 - 9$	40. $9 - 8$	41. $10 - 8$	42. $9 - 9$
43. $9 + 9$	44. $10 - 8$	45. $9 + 7$	46. $10 + 9$	47. $9 + 9$	48. $8 + 7$
49. $8 + 7$	50. $9 - 7$	51. $7 + 9$	52. $7 + 9$	53. $10 - 8$	54. $8 - 8$
55. $8 - 8$	56. $9 + 8$	57. $9 + 8$	58. $8 - 8$	59. $9 + 9$	60. $8 + 9$

1. $10 + 9$	2. $9 - 9$	3. $7 + 9$	4. $10 + 10$	5. $9 + 7$	6. $9 - 8$
7. $8 - 8$	8. $9 + 10$	9. $9 - 7$	10. $10 - 8$	11. $10 - 9$	12. $8 - 7$
13. $7 - 7$	14. $10 - 10$	15. $10 - 7$	16. $9 + 9$	17. $9 + 8$	18. $10 + 8$
19. $8 + 10$	20. $10 - 10$	21. $9 - 9$	22. $7 + 8$	23. $9 - 8$	24. $8 - 7$
25. $8 + 8$	26. $8 + 9$	27. $8 + 7$	28. $7 + 10$	29. $9 - 8$	30. $9 - 7$
31. $9 - 9$	32. $10 + 7$	33. $10 - 7$	34. $8 - 8$	35. $8 - 8$	36. $7 + 7$
37. $8 + 8$	38. $8 + 9$	39. $9 - 8$	40. $10 - 8$	41. $9 + 9$	42. $9 + 10$
43. $8 + 7$	44. $9 + 8$	45. $7 + 7$	46. $10 + 7$	47. $8 + 9$	48. $9 + 9$
49. $9 - 8$	50. $9 - 8$	51. $10 + 7$	52. $10 - 8$	53. $10 - 10$	54. $8 + 10$
55. $8 - 8$	56. $10 - 9$	57. $10 - 9$	58. $8 - 7$	59. $8 + 8$	60. $9 + 7$

1.   8
   + 6
	2. 10
	   + 0
		3. 9
		   + 18
			4. 11
			   - 8
				5. 9
				   + 19
					6. 9
					   + 2

7.   9
   - 9
	8. 17
	   - 8
		9. 10
		   + 19
			10. 17
			   - 10
				11. 10
				   - 9
					12. 9
					   + 4

13.   10
   + 5
	14. 7
	   + 13
		15. 8
		   + 9
			16. 15
			   - 7
				17. 9
				   + 16
					18. 9
					   + 15

19.   8
   + 4
	20. 15
	   - 10
		21. 15
		   - 9
			22. 12
			   - 9
				23. 14
				   - 10
					24. 12
					   - 8

25.   15
   - 8
	26. 9
	   + 14
		27. 8
		   + 3
			28. 13
			   - 9
				29. 11
				   - 9
					30. 19
					   - 10

31.   17
   - 7
	32. 8
	   - 8
		33. 13
		   - 10
			34. 9
			   - 7
				35. 10
				   - 8
					36. 10
					   + 2

37.   7
   + 5
	38. 14
	   - 8
		39. 7
		   + 8
			40. 17
			   - 9
				41. 9
				   + 10
					42. 7
					   + 16

43.   14
   - 7
	44. 18
	   - 8
		45. 9
		   + 5
			46. 9
			   + 13
				47. 7
				   + 10
					48. 9
					   + 12

49.   10
   - 10
	50. 14
	   - 9
		51. 8
		   - 7
			52. 8
			   + 18
				53. 13
				   - 7
					54. 16
					   - 8

55.   8
   + 13
	56. 8
	   + 15
		57. 18
		   - 9
			58. 8
			   + 2
				59. 8
				   + 19
					60. 9
					   + 3

1. 8 + 17	2. 14 - 7	3. 8 + 11	4. 8 + 13	5. 11 - 10	6. 12 - 8
7. 9 + 19	8. 18 - 8	9. 16 - 7	10. 10 - 10	11. 17 - 7	12. 12 - 7
13. 7 + 13	14. 9 + 8	15. 8 + 14	16. 19 - 8	17. 9 + 7	18. 10 - 9
19. 9 + 1	20. 10 + 15	21. 13 - 8	22. 8 + 6	23. 8 + 10	24. 10 - 8
25. 8 + 4	26. 15 - 7	27. 14 - 10	28. 11 - 9	29. 7 + 19	30. 8 + 8
31. 8 + 1	32. 9 + 12	33. 9 + 5	34. 17 - 10	35. 16 - 9	36. 9 + 14
37. 11 - 7	38. 14 - 8	39. 9 + 6	40. 7 + 18	41. 10 + 9	42. 8 - 8
43. 8 + 16	44. 19 - 10	45. 9 + 11	46. 16 - 8	47. 8 + 12	48. 18 - 7
49. 8 + 9	50. 12 - 9	51. 11 - 8	52. 8 + 2	53. 10 + 8	54. 18 - 10
55. 10 + 20	56. 13 - 9	57. 18 - 9	58. 10 + 16	59. 17 - 8	60. 9 - 7

Day 80
Adding and Subtracting

NAME: _______________   TIME: Score: /60

1. 11 − 8	2. 18 − 9	3. 19 − 9	4. 15 − 7	5. 9 + 13	6. 12 − 10
7. 20 − 8	8. 9 − 7	9. 8 + 7	10. 7 + 7	11. 7 + 1	12. 8 + 11
13. 7 + 10	14. 16 − 7	15. 11 − 9	16. 7 + 6	17. 18 − 7	18. 12 − 9
19. 17 − 9	20. 13 − 9	21. 9 + 3	22. 10 − 8	23. 14 − 9	24. 9 + 15
25. 20 − 7	26. 15 − 10	27. 15 − 8	28. 9 + 14	29. 7 + 5	30. 17 − 10
31. 9 + 8	32. 9 + 11	33. 7 − 7	34. 9 + 10	35. 12 − 8	36. 10 + 16
37. 9 + 12	38. 9 − 9	39. 9 + 17	40. 7 + 19	41. 16 − 8	42. 9 + 16
43. 11 − 7	44. 15 − 9	45. 10 + 14	46. 17 − 8	47. 10 − 9	48. 10 + 13
49. 18 − 10	50. 8 + 16	51. 8 − 8	52. 8 + 15	53. 10 + 12	54. 7 + 13
55. 9 + 2	56. 10 + 19	57. 10 − 10	58. 8 + 20	59. 9 + 1	60. 9 + 0

1. 15 − 8	2. 9 + 3	3. 8 + 8	4. 8 + 15	5. 9 + 20	6. 12 − 9
7. 17 − 8	8. 10 − 10	9. 13 − 8	10. 18 − 7	11. 10 − 9	12. 8 + 6
13. 9 + 2	14. 9 + 7	15. 19 − 9	16. 15 − 9	17. 8 + 14	18. 8 + 17
19. 14 − 7	20. 11 − 8	21. 10 + 8	22. 18 − 9	23. 8 + 12	24. 8 + 13
25. 9 + 14	26. 20 − 9	27. 20 − 10	28. 14 − 8	29. 11 − 10	30. 18 − 8
31. 12 − 8	32. 9 + 18	33. 9 + 5	34. 8 + 4	35. 10 + 3	36. 8 − 7
37. 18 − 10	38. 7 + 3	39. 19 − 7	40. 8 − 8	41. 10 + 2	42. 8 + 1
43. 9 − 7	44. 10 + 10	45. 8 + 16	46. 8 + 5	47. 19 − 10	48. 14 − 10
49. 10 + 18	50. 11 − 7	51. 8 + 20	52. 16 − 10	53. 8 + 11	54. 9 + 17
55. 19 − 8	56. 8 + 7	57. 10 + 17	58. 14 − 9	59. 9 + 12	60. 16 − 7

1. 18 − 8	2. 7 + 9	3. 8 − 7	4. 18 − 7	5. 19 − 8	6. 7 + 3
7. 12 − 9	8. 19 − 9	9. 7 + 10	10. 8 + 13	11. 20 − 9	12. 8 + 14
13. 9 − 9	14. 7 + 13	15. 11 − 10	16. 13 − 8	17. 10 + 18	18. 15 − 9
19. 9 + 13	20. 19 − 10	21. 9 + 3	22. 10 + 1	23. 12 − 8	24. 13 − 7
25. 20 − 8	26. 19 − 7	27. 7 + 18	28. 11 − 8	29. 9 + 2	30. 14 − 8
31. 8 + 9	32. 9 − 8	33. 8 + 19	34. 9 + 7	35. 10 + 16	36. 8 + 10
37. 10 − 10	38. 9 + 9	39. 17 − 9	40. 14 − 7	41. 9 − 7	42. 7 + 15
43. 7 + 2	44. 8 + 1	45. 18 − 10	46. 8 + 0	47. 17 − 10	48. 9 + 15
49. 7 − 7	50. 8 + 5	51. 8 − 8	52. 10 − 8	53. 10 + 19	54. 10 + 12
55. 7 + 8	56. 9 + 6	57. 8 + 7	58. 13 − 9	59. 7 + 11	60. 13 − 10

Day 83
Adding and Subtracting

NAME: ___________   TIME: Score: /60

1. 9 + 13	2. 9 + 10	3. 8 − 8	4. 15 − 8	5. 13 − 7	6. 8 + 5
7. 9 + 19	8. 16 − 8	9. 7 + 11	10. 10 − 8	11. 8 + 12	12. 7 + 5
13. 17 − 8	14. 8 + 15	15. 9 + 7	16. 10 + 14	17. 12 − 10	18. 14 − 8
19. 18 − 8	20. 11 − 9	21. 12 − 9	22. 9 + 15	23. 17 − 9	24. 12 − 8
25. 9 + 11	26. 8 + 11	27. 13 − 8	28. 10 + 5	29. 8 + 7	30. 15 − 7
31. 8 + 3	32. 14 − 7	33. 8 + 13	34. 7 + 7	35. 14 − 9	36. 15 − 10
37. 18 − 9	38. 10 − 9	39. 8 + 10	40. 18 − 10	41. 13 − 9	42. 19 − 8
43. 19 − 9	44. 10 + 0	45. 8 + 6	46. 10 + 11	47. 8 + 1	48. 8 + 16
49. 17 − 10	50. 9 − 8	51. 9 − 7	52. 9 + 6	53. 7 + 16	54. 7 + 4
55. 8 + 14	56. 15 − 9	57. 20 − 9	58. 9 − 9	59. 10 + 6	60. 7 + 17

1. $13 - 9$	2. $9 + 7$	3. $15 - 7$	4. $8 + 14$	5. $10 - 9$	6. $15 - 9$
7. $7 + 11$	8. $10 + 15$	9. $10 - 7$	10. $16 - 8$	11. $9 - 7$	12. $18 - 10$
13. $15 - 10$	14. $7 + 0$	15. $17 - 7$	16. $11 - 9$	17. $9 + 16$	18. $9 + 2$
19. $8 + 1$	20. $14 - 8$	21. $7 + 3$	22. $16 - 9$	23. $18 - 8$	24. $9 + 4$
25. $9 + 8$	26. $12 - 10$	27. $8 + 9$	28. $9 - 8$	29. $10 - 10$	30. $7 + 15$
31. $8 + 16$	32. $11 - 7$	33. $9 - 9$	34. $12 - 8$	35. $8 + 6$	36. $10 + 3$
37. $19 - 8$	38. $7 + 4$	39. $9 + 5$	40. $20 - 9$	41. $9 + 17$	42. $11 - 8$
43. $7 + 8$	44. $15 - 8$	45. $10 + 14$	46. $10 + 0$	47. $9 + 6$	48. $20 - 10$
49. $7 + 1$	50. $17 - 10$	51. $17 - 9$	52. $9 + 19$	53. $17 - 8$	54. $8 + 7$
55. $10 - 8$	56. $10 + 18$	57. $7 + 7$	58. $9 + 11$	59. $8 + 15$	60. $12 - 9$

1.	2.	3.	4.	5.	6.
15 − 9	9 + 6	9 + 10	10 + 17	9 + 11	8 − 7

7.	8.	9.	10.	11.	12.
17 − 10	8 + 16	7 + 19	9 + 18	12 − 10	19 − 9

13.	14.	15.	16.	17.	18.
13 − 9	9 + 20	16 − 9	15 − 8	9 + 19	17 − 8

19.	20.	21.	22.	23.	24.
9 + 9	11 − 10	8 + 12	18 − 10	8 + 8	9 − 9

25.	26.	27.	28.	29.	30.
11 − 7	8 + 17	9 − 8	20 − 7	9 + 13	12 − 8

31.	32.	33.	34.	35.	36.
20 − 9	9 + 5	9 + 4	18 − 9	10 + 7	18 − 7

37.	38.	39.	40.	41.	42.
8 + 13	8 + 19	7 + 9	12 − 7	17 − 9	8 + 6

43.	44.	45.	46.	47.	48.
8 + 18	11 − 8	10 + 20	14 − 9	8 + 14	7 + 6

49.	50.	51.	52.	53.	54.
11 − 9	9 + 7	8 + 10	10 − 8	8 + 9	19 − 7

55.	56.	57.	58.	59.	60.
19 − 8	8 + 11	13 − 8	18 − 8	9 + 1	16 − 8

1. $\begin{array}{r} 7 \\ +\ 18 \\ \hline \end{array}$	2. $\begin{array}{r} 9 \\ +\ 8 \\ \hline \end{array}$	3. $\begin{array}{r} 9 \\ +\ 19 \\ \hline \end{array}$	4. $\begin{array}{r} 9 \\ +\ 14 \\ \hline \end{array}$	5. $\begin{array}{r} 10 \\ +\ 18 \\ \hline \end{array}$	6. $\begin{array}{r} 13 \\ -\ 9 \\ \hline \end{array}$
7. $\begin{array}{r} 17 \\ -\ 7 \\ \hline \end{array}$	8. $\begin{array}{r} 16 \\ -\ 9 \\ \hline \end{array}$	9. $\begin{array}{r} 9 \\ +\ 16 \\ \hline \end{array}$	10. $\begin{array}{r} 14 \\ -\ 9 \\ \hline \end{array}$	11. $\begin{array}{r} 13 \\ -\ 8 \\ \hline \end{array}$	12. $\begin{array}{r} 7 \\ +\ 14 \\ \hline \end{array}$
13. $\begin{array}{r} 8 \\ -\ 8 \\ \hline \end{array}$	14. $\begin{array}{r} 9 \\ +\ 13 \\ \hline \end{array}$	15. $\begin{array}{r} 8 \\ +\ 11 \\ \hline \end{array}$	16. $\begin{array}{r} 18 \\ -\ 8 \\ \hline \end{array}$	17. $\begin{array}{r} 9 \\ -\ 8 \\ \hline \end{array}$	18. $\begin{array}{r} 12 \\ -\ 7 \\ \hline \end{array}$
19. $\begin{array}{r} 11 \\ -\ 9 \\ \hline \end{array}$	20. $\begin{array}{r} 18 \\ -\ 10 \\ \hline \end{array}$	21. $\begin{array}{r} 15 \\ -\ 10 \\ \hline \end{array}$	22. $\begin{array}{r} 8 \\ +\ 4 \\ \hline \end{array}$	23. $\begin{array}{r} 19 \\ -\ 9 \\ \hline \end{array}$	24. $\begin{array}{r} 20 \\ -\ 8 \\ \hline \end{array}$
25. $\begin{array}{r} 7 \\ +\ 3 \\ \hline \end{array}$	26. $\begin{array}{r} 19 \\ -\ 10 \\ \hline \end{array}$	27. $\begin{array}{r} 20 \\ -\ 9 \\ \hline \end{array}$	28. $\begin{array}{r} 14 \\ -\ 8 \\ \hline \end{array}$	29. $\begin{array}{r} 12 \\ -\ 9 \\ \hline \end{array}$	30. $\begin{array}{r} 10 \\ +\ 8 \\ \hline \end{array}$
31. $\begin{array}{r} 10 \\ +\ 10 \\ \hline \end{array}$	32. $\begin{array}{r} 7 \\ +\ 13 \\ \hline \end{array}$	33. $\begin{array}{r} 16 \\ -\ 8 \\ \hline \end{array}$	34. $\begin{array}{r} 8 \\ +\ 3 \\ \hline \end{array}$	35. $\begin{array}{r} 9 \\ +\ 4 \\ \hline \end{array}$	36. $\begin{array}{r} 8 \\ +\ 12 \\ \hline \end{array}$
37. $\begin{array}{r} 15 \\ -\ 8 \\ \hline \end{array}$	38. $\begin{array}{r} 7 \\ +\ 2 \\ \hline \end{array}$	39. $\begin{array}{r} 9 \\ +\ 6 \\ \hline \end{array}$	40. $\begin{array}{r} 8 \\ +\ 17 \\ \hline \end{array}$	41. $\begin{array}{r} 7 \\ +\ 10 \\ \hline \end{array}$	42. $\begin{array}{r} 11 \\ -\ 8 \\ \hline \end{array}$
43. $\begin{array}{r} 18 \\ -\ 9 \\ \hline \end{array}$	44. $\begin{array}{r} 10 \\ -\ 9 \\ \hline \end{array}$	45. $\begin{array}{r} 9 \\ +\ 9 \\ \hline \end{array}$	46. $\begin{array}{r} 7 \\ +\ 19 \\ \hline \end{array}$	47. $\begin{array}{r} 10 \\ +\ 5 \\ \hline \end{array}$	48. $\begin{array}{r} 12 \\ -\ 10 \\ \hline \end{array}$
49. $\begin{array}{r} 10 \\ +\ 12 \\ \hline \end{array}$	50. $\begin{array}{r} 8 \\ +\ 10 \\ \hline \end{array}$	51. $\begin{array}{r} 7 \\ +\ 17 \\ \hline \end{array}$	52. $\begin{array}{r} 10 \\ -\ 7 \\ \hline \end{array}$	53. $\begin{array}{r} 9 \\ +\ 17 \\ \hline \end{array}$	54. $\begin{array}{r} 9 \\ +\ 5 \\ \hline \end{array}$
55. $\begin{array}{r} 19 \\ -\ 7 \\ \hline \end{array}$	56. $\begin{array}{r} 9 \\ +\ 20 \\ \hline \end{array}$	57. $\begin{array}{r} 9 \\ -\ 7 \\ \hline \end{array}$	58. $\begin{array}{r} 17 \\ -\ 9 \\ \hline \end{array}$	59. $\begin{array}{r} 18 \\ -\ 7 \\ \hline \end{array}$	60. $\begin{array}{r} 19 \\ -\ 8 \\ \hline \end{array}$

1. 14 − 8	2. 15 − 10	3. 9 + 14	4. 10 + 4	5. 7 + 4	6. 8 + 8
7. 17 − 10	8. 7 + 5	9. 11 − 8	10. 10 − 9	11. 17 − 8	12. 8 + 3
13. 8 + 12	14. 8 + 6	15. 8 + 5	16. 10 + 13	17. 9 + 18	18. 9 + 4
19. 8 + 15	20. 7 − 7	21. 11 − 7	22. 9 + 17	23. 18 − 7	24. 10 − 8
25. 10 + 14	26. 7 + 9	27. 19 − 7	28. 11 − 10	29. 13 − 10	30. 9 − 7
31. 7 + 18	32. 7 + 19	33. 13 − 8	34. 9 + 10	35. 8 + 19	36. 8 + 11
37. 9 + 15	38. 16 − 8	39. 9 − 8	40. 8 + 16	41. 14 − 9	42. 18 − 10
43. 9 + 20	44. 13 − 9	45. 20 − 8	46. 19 − 8	47. 19 − 9	48. 8 − 8
49. 12 − 8	50. 17 − 9	51. 8 − 7	52. 15 − 8	53. 8 + 18	54. 10 + 1
55. 16 − 9	56. 9 + 16	57. 10 + 5	58. 16 − 7	59. 8 + 1	60. 7 + 7

1. 10 - 8	2. 7 + 19	3. 10 + 3	4. 15 - 10	5. 8 + 1	6. 9 + 11
7. 13 - 7	8. 8 + 12	9. 19 - 9	10. 16 - 8	11. 9 + 10	12. 8 + 15
13. 16 - 10	14. 15 - 8	15. 9 + 16	16. 8 - 8	17. 8 + 9	18. 10 - 7
19. 8 + 11	20. 19 - 10	21. 8 + 4	22. 18 - 8	23. 8 + 10	24. 20 - 9
25. 19 - 7	26. 16 - 9	27. 7 + 9	28. 10 + 11	29. 12 - 7	30. 18 - 9
31. 10 + 4	32. 18 - 10	33. 9 - 8	34. 9 + 4	35. 12 - 9	36. 10 + 10
37. 13 - 9	38. 8 + 13	39. 10 + 13	40. 9 + 0	41. 17 - 9	42. 9 + 1
43. 14 - 7	44. 8 + 14	45. 8 + 17	46. 10 + 8	47. 15 - 7	48. 8 + 16
49. 10 - 9	50. 9 + 14	51. 20 - 8	52. 9 + 17	53. 14 - 8	54. 14 - 9
55. 10 + 2	56. 12 - 10	57. 19 - 8	58. 13 - 8	59. 9 + 15	60. 9 + 19

1. 8 − 8	2. 8 + 0	3. 8 + 19	4. 17 − 9	5. 9 − 9	6. 8 + 17
7. 8 − 7	8. 10 − 10	9. 8 + 5	10. 10 + 12	11. 14 − 7	12. 7 + 10
13. 18 − 10	14. 12 − 9	15. 10 − 8	16. 10 + 13	17. 9 + 8	18. 8 + 2
19. 16 − 9	20. 9 + 6	21. 13 − 9	22. 20 − 8	23. 17 − 10	24. 11 − 8
25. 9 + 17	26. 9 + 11	27. 8 + 4	28. 16 − 7	29. 9 − 8	30. 8 + 10
31. 13 − 10	32. 17 − 7	33. 15 − 10	34. 14 − 8	35. 7 + 12	36. 9 + 0
37. 9 + 5	38. 8 + 7	39. 16 − 8	40. 15 − 8	41. 9 − 7	42. 18 − 9
43. 9 + 18	44. 15 − 9	45. 9 + 15	46. 9 + 7	47. 12 − 7	48. 19 − 9
49. 19 − 8	50. 9 + 16	51. 7 + 16	52. 9 + 12	53. 9 + 1	54. 10 + 2
55. 10 + 14	56. 17 − 8	57. 8 + 6	58. 10 + 11	59. 8 + 18	60. 11 − 9

NAME: __________   TIME: Score: /60

1. 12 − 9	2. 8 + 18	3. 7 + 4	4. 9 + 18	5. 8 + 15	6. 15 − 9
7. 8 + 11	8. 8 − 7	9. 9 + 8	10. 8 + 13	11. 18 − 8	12. 13 − 9
13. 18 − 9	14. 9 + 6	15. 16 − 9	16. 8 + 16	17. 10 + 6	18. 15 − 8
19. 10 + 0	20. 16 − 8	21. 17 − 8	22. 19 − 8	23. 8 + 9	24. 9 + 10
25. 9 + 4	26. 8 + 17	27. 9 − 9	28. 10 − 7	29. 15 − 7	30. 7 + 14
31. 10 − 8	32. 7 + 1	33. 9 + 13	34. 8 + 1	35. 8 − 8	36. 8 + 7
37. 12 − 8	38. 8 + 19	39. 10 + 8	40. 9 + 7	41. 11 − 10	42. 14 − 7
43. 8 + 2	44. 9 + 9	45. 13 − 8	46. 13 − 7	47. 11 − 9	48. 19 − 9
49. 14 − 9	50. 15 − 10	51. 20 − 9	52. 16 − 10	53. 10 + 2	54. 9 + 5
55. 7 + 19	56. 20 − 8	57. 11 − 7	58. 7 + 6	59. 8 + 14	60. 18 − 7

1. 8 + 1	2. 10 + 15	3. 13 - 10	4. 13 - 8	5. 10 + 2	6. 9 - 8
7. 10 + 4	8. 9 + 9	9. 8 + 11	10. 10 - 9	11. 9 + 10	12. 19 - 8
13. 8 + 4	14. 12 - 9	15. 9 + 12	16. 13 - 7	17. 16 - 9	18. 9 + 4
19. 9 + 5	20. 17 - 8	21. 11 - 10	22. 9 + 13	23. 9 + 1	24. 9 + 2
25. 13 - 9	26. 17 - 9	27. 18 - 7	28. 8 + 6	29. 10 + 7	30. 16 - 7
31. 8 + 2	32. 9 + 16	33. 17 - 7	34. 7 + 13	35. 7 + 8	36. 8 - 8
37. 8 + 0	38. 19 - 9	39. 9 + 7	40. 8 + 16	41. 15 - 9	42. 18 - 8
43. 11 - 9	44. 10 + 5	45. 15 - 8	46. 16 - 10	47. 12 - 10	48. 10 + 18
49. 10 + 9	50. 9 + 17	51. 16 - 8	52. 11 - 7	53. 7 - 7	54. 14 - 10
55. 7 + 9	56. 14 - 7	57. 19 - 7	58. 12 - 7	59. 10 + 13	60. 8 + 18

NAME: _______________   TIME: Score: /60

1. 9 + 4	2. 9 + 10	3. 9 + 14	4. 8 + 11	5. 9 + 1	6. 18 − 9
7. 9 + 13	8. 8 + 6	9. 11 − 8	10. 9 + 5	11. 8 + 18	12. 19 − 8
13. 9 + 17	14. 8 + 14	15. 16 − 7	16. 7 + 13	17. 10 − 9	18. 14 − 8
19. 13 − 7	20. 20 − 9	21. 18 − 7	22. 10 + 3	23. 9 + 2	24. 10 + 17
25. 10 − 8	26. 14 − 9	27. 16 − 9	28. 18 − 8	29. 18 − 10	30. 7 + 8
31. 8 + 20	32. 10 − 7	33. 10 + 18	34. 10 + 5	35. 7 + 2	36. 15 − 8
37. 14 − 7	38. 8 − 7	39. 11 − 9	40. 8 + 5	41. 13 − 10	42. 7 + 14
43. 20 − 8	44. 15 − 9	45. 8 − 8	46. 9 − 8	47. 9 + 11	48. 8 + 8
49. 8 + 9	50. 7 + 18	51. 15 − 10	52. 17 − 7	53. 7 + 7	54. 17 − 8
55. 9 + 16	56. 12 − 7	57. 9 + 9	58. 9 + 15	59. 7 − 7	60. 19 − 10

1. 16 − 10	2. 7 + 1	3. 20 − 8	4. 12 − 9	5. 10 − 9	6. 18 − 8
7. 9 + 19	8. 19 − 8	9. 15 − 8	10. 18 − 7	11. 7 + 3	12. 9 + 3
13. 14 − 8	14. 9 + 10	15. 11 − 9	16. 12 − 10	17. 17 − 7	18. 12 − 8
19. 9 − 9	20. 8 + 1	21. 19 − 9	22. 8 + 13	23. 15 − 9	24. 8 + 12
25. 8 + 11	26. 9 + 1	27. 8 + 8	28. 10 + 4	29. 8 + 4	30. 14 − 9
31. 9 + 15	32. 9 + 2	33. 9 + 17	34. 8 − 8	35. 10 − 7	36. 9 − 8
37. 16 − 7	38. 18 − 9	39. 10 + 12	40. 18 − 10	41. 9 + 14	42. 17 − 9
43. 10 + 3	44. 8 + 6	45. 11 − 10	46. 16 − 8	47. 15 − 7	48. 20 − 7
49. 9 + 7	50. 8 + 7	51. 7 + 17	52. 8 + 10	53. 9 + 13	54. 16 − 9
55. 8 + 9	56. 10 + 9	57. 10 + 13	58. 7 + 13	59. 17 − 10	60. 8 + 14

1. 9 + 17	2. 10 + 16	3. 7 + 16	4. 8 + 20	5. 16 - 9	6. 14 - 8
7. 10 + 0	8. 8 - 8	9. 12 - 9	10. 7 + 1	11. 10 + 3	12. 7 + 12
13. 19 - 9	14. 14 - 9	15. 8 + 3	16. 15 - 9	17. 10 + 10	18. 10 - 9
19. 12 - 8	20. 8 - 7	21. 9 - 9	22. 19 - 8	23. 8 + 2	24. 9 + 12
25. 18 - 8	26. 15 - 8	27. 13 - 7	28. 9 + 6	29. 17 - 8	30. 7 + 13
31. 10 + 2	32. 8 + 16	33. 9 + 9	34. 15 - 10	35. 8 + 7	36. 7 + 19
37. 18 - 9	38. 13 - 8	39. 7 + 11	40. 10 - 8	41. 8 + 18	42. 15 - 7
43. 18 - 7	44. 9 + 10	45. 10 + 14	46. 13 - 10	47. 8 + 4	48. 20 - 9
49. 8 + 8	50. 8 + 6	51. 9 + 14	52. 11 - 9	53. 11 - 10	54. 17 - 7
55. 20 - 8	56. 12 - 10	57. 17 - 9	58. 7 + 17	59. 9 + 5	60. 8 + 11

Day 95
Adding and Subtracting

NAME:________ TIME: Score: /60

1. 8 + 10	2. 17 − 7	3. 17 − 8	4. 10 − 8	5. 16 − 7	6. 11 − 8
7. 9 + 8	8. 19 − 8	9. 8 + 11	10. 11 − 7	11. 8 + 13	12. 12 − 10
13. 14 − 9	14. 8 + 4	15. 7 + 9	16. 10 + 2	17. 9 + 3	18. 8 + 19
19. 13 − 9	20. 12 − 8	21. 10 − 9	22. 16 − 8	23. 8 + 2	24. 7 + 10
25. 15 − 9	26. 10 + 10	27. 10 + 4	28. 9 + 12	29. 10 + 19	30. 9 + 13
31. 12 − 9	32. 8 − 8	33. 9 + 14	34. 10 + 18	35. 7 + 0	36. 20 − 7
37. 14 − 7	38. 19 − 7	39. 10 + 5	40. 12 − 7	41. 8 + 9	42. 18 − 8
43. 13 − 7	44. 15 − 8	45. 9 − 8	46. 8 + 12	47. 9 + 17	48. 17 − 10
49. 8 + 17	50. 20 − 8	51. 20 − 9	52. 9 + 4	53. 8 + 3	54. 9 + 11
55. 13 − 10	56. 9 + 5	57. 8 + 16	58. 9 − 9	59. 10 + 7	60. 10 − 7

1. $\begin{array}{r} 10 \\ -\ 10 \\ \hline \end{array}$	2. $\begin{array}{r} 10 \\ -\ 8 \\ \hline \end{array}$	3. $\begin{array}{r} 9 \\ +\ 1 \\ \hline \end{array}$	4. $\begin{array}{r} 8 \\ +\ 3 \\ \hline \end{array}$	5. $\begin{array}{r} 7 \\ -\ 7 \\ \hline \end{array}$	6. $\begin{array}{r} 9 \\ +\ 13 \\ \hline \end{array}$
7. $\begin{array}{r} 20 \\ -\ 9 \\ \hline \end{array}$	8. $\begin{array}{r} 8 \\ +\ 1 \\ \hline \end{array}$	9. $\begin{array}{r} 14 \\ -\ 9 \\ \hline \end{array}$	10. $\begin{array}{r} 16 \\ -\ 7 \\ \hline \end{array}$	11. $\begin{array}{r} 13 \\ -\ 8 \\ \hline \end{array}$	12. $\begin{array}{r} 18 \\ -\ 9 \\ \hline \end{array}$
13. $\begin{array}{r} 11 \\ -\ 8 \\ \hline \end{array}$	14. $\begin{array}{r} 8 \\ +\ 11 \\ \hline \end{array}$	15. $\begin{array}{r} 15 \\ -\ 9 \\ \hline \end{array}$	16. $\begin{array}{r} 19 \\ -\ 10 \\ \hline \end{array}$	17. $\begin{array}{r} 10 \\ +\ 14 \\ \hline \end{array}$	18. $\begin{array}{r} 8 \\ +\ 6 \\ \hline \end{array}$
19. $\begin{array}{r} 18 \\ -\ 10 \\ \hline \end{array}$	20. $\begin{array}{r} 19 \\ -\ 8 \\ \hline \end{array}$	21. $\begin{array}{r} 13 \\ -\ 9 \\ \hline \end{array}$	22. $\begin{array}{r} 17 \\ -\ 7 \\ \hline \end{array}$	23. $\begin{array}{r} 17 \\ -\ 9 \\ \hline \end{array}$	24. $\begin{array}{r} 9 \\ +\ 19 \\ \hline \end{array}$
25. $\begin{array}{r} 9 \\ +\ 2 \\ \hline \end{array}$	26. $\begin{array}{r} 17 \\ -\ 8 \\ \hline \end{array}$	27. $\begin{array}{r} 7 \\ +\ 11 \\ \hline \end{array}$	28. $\begin{array}{r} 13 \\ -\ 10 \\ \hline \end{array}$	29. $\begin{array}{r} 10 \\ +\ 16 \\ \hline \end{array}$	30. $\begin{array}{r} 9 \\ -\ 7 \\ \hline \end{array}$
31. $\begin{array}{r} 10 \\ +\ 9 \\ \hline \end{array}$	32. $\begin{array}{r} 9 \\ +\ 15 \\ \hline \end{array}$	33. $\begin{array}{r} 18 \\ -\ 7 \\ \hline \end{array}$	34. $\begin{array}{r} 8 \\ -\ 8 \\ \hline \end{array}$	35. $\begin{array}{r} 11 \\ -\ 10 \\ \hline \end{array}$	36. $\begin{array}{r} 12 \\ -\ 7 \\ \hline \end{array}$
37. $\begin{array}{r} 8 \\ +\ 5 \\ \hline \end{array}$	38. $\begin{array}{r} 10 \\ -\ 7 \\ \hline \end{array}$	39. $\begin{array}{r} 9 \\ +\ 9 \\ \hline \end{array}$	40. $\begin{array}{r} 16 \\ -\ 8 \\ \hline \end{array}$	41. $\begin{array}{r} 7 \\ +\ 4 \\ \hline \end{array}$	42. $\begin{array}{r} 9 \\ +\ 6 \\ \hline \end{array}$
43. $\begin{array}{r} 7 \\ +\ 5 \\ \hline \end{array}$	44. $\begin{array}{r} 9 \\ +\ 5 \\ \hline \end{array}$	45. $\begin{array}{r} 8 \\ +\ 17 \\ \hline \end{array}$	46. $\begin{array}{r} 8 \\ +\ 10 \\ \hline \end{array}$	47. $\begin{array}{r} 12 \\ -\ 8 \\ \hline \end{array}$	48. $\begin{array}{r} 10 \\ +\ 17 \\ \hline \end{array}$
49. $\begin{array}{r} 8 \\ +\ 18 \\ \hline \end{array}$	50. $\begin{array}{r} 8 \\ +\ 20 \\ \hline \end{array}$	51. $\begin{array}{r} 10 \\ +\ 8 \\ \hline \end{array}$	52. $\begin{array}{r} 9 \\ +\ 14 \\ \hline \end{array}$	53. $\begin{array}{r} 15 \\ -\ 8 \\ \hline \end{array}$	54. $\begin{array}{r} 12 \\ -\ 9 \\ \hline \end{array}$
55. $\begin{array}{r} 10 \\ +\ 10 \\ \hline \end{array}$	56. $\begin{array}{r} 9 \\ +\ 11 \\ \hline \end{array}$	57. $\begin{array}{r} 11 \\ -\ 9 \\ \hline \end{array}$	58. $\begin{array}{r} 20 \\ -\ 10 \\ \hline \end{array}$	59. $\begin{array}{r} 8 \\ +\ 12 \\ \hline \end{array}$	60. $\begin{array}{r} 7 \\ +\ 13 \\ \hline \end{array}$

Day 97
Adding and Subtracting

NAME: ___________ TIME: Score: /60

1. $9 + 6$	2. $8 + 14$	3. $7 + 17$	4. $8 + 5$	5. $15 - 8$	6. $7 + 4$
7. $10 - 8$	8. $13 - 8$	9. $9 - 9$	10. $19 - 8$	11. $10 + 13$	12. $7 + 6$
13. $18 - 8$	14. $9 + 17$	15. $7 + 7$	16. $7 + 1$	17. $16 - 8$	18. $14 - 9$
19. $9 + 11$	20. $8 + 1$	21. $10 + 18$	22. $9 + 13$	23. $9 + 10$	24. $8 + 15$
25. $16 - 10$	26. $8 - 8$	27. $20 - 7$	28. $14 - 8$	29. $9 - 8$	30. $17 - 8$
31. $12 - 9$	32. $8 + 6$	33. $18 - 10$	34. $8 + 12$	35. $11 - 9$	36. $9 + 5$
37. $11 - 8$	38. $7 + 2$	39. $9 - 7$	40. $8 - 7$	41. $7 + 8$	42. $9 + 14$
43. $17 - 10$	44. $7 + 3$	45. $14 - 10$	46. $8 + 4$	47. $16 - 9$	48. $10 + 8$
49. $9 + 3$	50. $10 + 15$	51. $9 + 8$	52. $19 - 9$	53. $13 - 10$	54. $18 - 9$
55. $13 - 9$	56. $9 + 0$	57. $17 - 9$	58. $12 - 7$	59. $14 - 7$	60. $9 + 9$

1. $\begin{array}{r} 17 \\ -\ 7 \\ \hline \end{array}$	2. $\begin{array}{r} 9 \\ +\ 12 \\ \hline \end{array}$	3. $\begin{array}{r} 19 \\ -\ 8 \\ \hline \end{array}$	4. $\begin{array}{r} 12 \\ -\ 8 \\ \hline \end{array}$	5. $\begin{array}{r} 9 \\ +\ 1 \\ \hline \end{array}$	6. $\begin{array}{r} 8 \\ +\ 6 \\ \hline \end{array}$
7. $\begin{array}{r} 9 \\ -\ 8 \\ \hline \end{array}$	8. $\begin{array}{r} 12 \\ -\ 10 \\ \hline \end{array}$	9. $\begin{array}{r} 9 \\ +\ 10 \\ \hline \end{array}$	10. $\begin{array}{r} 19 \\ -\ 9 \\ \hline \end{array}$	11. $\begin{array}{r} 7 \\ +\ 20 \\ \hline \end{array}$	12. $\begin{array}{r} 9 \\ +\ 11 \\ \hline \end{array}$
13. $\begin{array}{r} 8 \\ +\ 10 \\ \hline \end{array}$	14. $\begin{array}{r} 8 \\ -\ 8 \\ \hline \end{array}$	15. $\begin{array}{r} 11 \\ -\ 9 \\ \hline \end{array}$	16. $\begin{array}{r} 14 \\ -\ 8 \\ \hline \end{array}$	17. $\begin{array}{r} 15 \\ -\ 8 \\ \hline \end{array}$	18. $\begin{array}{r} 8 \\ +\ 7 \\ \hline \end{array}$
19. $\begin{array}{r} 8 \\ +\ 20 \\ \hline \end{array}$	20. $\begin{array}{r} 10 \\ +\ 19 \\ \hline \end{array}$	21. $\begin{array}{r} 16 \\ -\ 9 \\ \hline \end{array}$	22. $\begin{array}{r} 20 \\ -\ 8 \\ \hline \end{array}$	23. $\begin{array}{r} 7 \\ +\ 13 \\ \hline \end{array}$	24. $\begin{array}{r} 9 \\ +\ 5 \\ \hline \end{array}$
25. $\begin{array}{r} 9 \\ -\ 9 \\ \hline \end{array}$	26. $\begin{array}{r} 10 \\ +\ 9 \\ \hline \end{array}$	27. $\begin{array}{r} 8 \\ +\ 18 \\ \hline \end{array}$	28. $\begin{array}{r} 17 \\ -\ 9 \\ \hline \end{array}$	29. $\begin{array}{r} 10 \\ +\ 4 \\ \hline \end{array}$	30. $\begin{array}{r} 10 \\ -\ 8 \\ \hline \end{array}$
31. $\begin{array}{r} 7 \\ +\ 12 \\ \hline \end{array}$	32. $\begin{array}{r} 9 \\ +\ 13 \\ \hline \end{array}$	33. $\begin{array}{r} 15 \\ -\ 7 \\ \hline \end{array}$	34. $\begin{array}{r} 10 \\ -\ 9 \\ \hline \end{array}$	35. $\begin{array}{r} 8 \\ +\ 19 \\ \hline \end{array}$	36. $\begin{array}{r} 10 \\ +\ 16 \\ \hline \end{array}$
37. $\begin{array}{r} 18 \\ -\ 7 \\ \hline \end{array}$	38. $\begin{array}{r} 10 \\ +\ 3 \\ \hline \end{array}$	39. $\begin{array}{r} 7 \\ +\ 17 \\ \hline \end{array}$	40. $\begin{array}{r} 18 \\ -\ 8 \\ \hline \end{array}$	41. $\begin{array}{r} 8 \\ +\ 14 \\ \hline \end{array}$	42. $\begin{array}{r} 13 \\ -\ 9 \\ \hline \end{array}$
43. $\begin{array}{r} 13 \\ -\ 7 \\ \hline \end{array}$	44. $\begin{array}{r} 9 \\ +\ 14 \\ \hline \end{array}$	45. $\begin{array}{r} 9 \\ +\ 18 \\ \hline \end{array}$	46. $\begin{array}{r} 10 \\ -\ 7 \\ \hline \end{array}$	47. $\begin{array}{r} 7 \\ +\ 3 \\ \hline \end{array}$	48. $\begin{array}{r} 17 \\ -\ 8 \\ \hline \end{array}$
49. $\begin{array}{r} 14 \\ -\ 9 \\ \hline \end{array}$	50. $\begin{array}{r} 20 \\ -\ 10 \\ \hline \end{array}$	51. $\begin{array}{r} 16 \\ -\ 8 \\ \hline \end{array}$	52. $\begin{array}{r} 8 \\ +\ 13 \\ \hline \end{array}$	53. $\begin{array}{r} 9 \\ +\ 17 \\ \hline \end{array}$	54. $\begin{array}{r} 9 \\ +\ 19 \\ \hline \end{array}$
55. $\begin{array}{r} 15 \\ -\ 10 \\ \hline \end{array}$	56. $\begin{array}{r} 9 \\ +\ 9 \\ \hline \end{array}$	57. $\begin{array}{r} 18 \\ -\ 9 \\ \hline \end{array}$	58. $\begin{array}{r} 20 \\ -\ 7 \\ \hline \end{array}$	59. $\begin{array}{r} 9 \\ +\ 7 \\ \hline \end{array}$	60. $\begin{array}{r} 8 \\ -\ 7 \\ \hline \end{array}$

Day 99

Adding and Subtracting

1. $\begin{array}{r} 17 \\ -\ 9 \\ \hline \end{array}$	2. $\begin{array}{r} 15 \\ -\ 9 \\ \hline \end{array}$	3. $\begin{array}{r} 8 \\ +\ 13 \\ \hline \end{array}$	4. $\begin{array}{r} 10 \\ +\ 8 \\ \hline \end{array}$	5. $\begin{array}{r} 10 \\ +\ 4 \\ \hline \end{array}$	6. $\begin{array}{r} 9 \\ +\ 3 \\ \hline \end{array}$
7. $\begin{array}{r} 9 \\ +\ 2 \\ \hline \end{array}$	8. $\begin{array}{r} 20 \\ -\ 10 \\ \hline \end{array}$	9. $\begin{array}{r} 14 \\ -\ 9 \\ \hline \end{array}$	10. $\begin{array}{r} 9 \\ +\ 19 \\ \hline \end{array}$	11. $\begin{array}{r} 9 \\ -\ 9 \\ \hline \end{array}$	12. $\begin{array}{r} 14 \\ -\ 7 \\ \hline \end{array}$
13. $\begin{array}{r} 20 \\ -\ 9 \\ \hline \end{array}$	14. $\begin{array}{r} 10 \\ +\ 10 \\ \hline \end{array}$	15. $\begin{array}{r} 7 \\ +\ 7 \\ \hline \end{array}$	16. $\begin{array}{r} 10 \\ -\ 8 \\ \hline \end{array}$	17. $\begin{array}{r} 18 \\ -\ 9 \\ \hline \end{array}$	18. $\begin{array}{r} 13 \\ -\ 9 \\ \hline \end{array}$
19. $\begin{array}{r} 9 \\ +\ 18 \\ \hline \end{array}$	20. $\begin{array}{r} 9 \\ +\ 15 \\ \hline \end{array}$	21. $\begin{array}{r} 20 \\ -\ 8 \\ \hline \end{array}$	22. $\begin{array}{r} 10 \\ +\ 9 \\ \hline \end{array}$	23. $\begin{array}{r} 7 \\ +\ 3 \\ \hline \end{array}$	24. $\begin{array}{r} 9 \\ +\ 11 \\ \hline \end{array}$
25. $\begin{array}{r} 19 \\ -\ 8 \\ \hline \end{array}$	26. $\begin{array}{r} 11 \\ -\ 8 \\ \hline \end{array}$	27. $\begin{array}{r} 9 \\ +\ 5 \\ \hline \end{array}$	28. $\begin{array}{r} 7 \\ +\ 18 \\ \hline \end{array}$	29. $\begin{array}{r} 10 \\ -\ 7 \\ \hline \end{array}$	30. $\begin{array}{r} 13 \\ -\ 10 \\ \hline \end{array}$
31. $\begin{array}{r} 17 \\ -\ 8 \\ \hline \end{array}$	32. $\begin{array}{r} 10 \\ +\ 3 \\ \hline \end{array}$	33. $\begin{array}{r} 14 \\ -\ 10 \\ \hline \end{array}$	34. $\begin{array}{r} 8 \\ +\ 9 \\ \hline \end{array}$	35. $\begin{array}{r} 18 \\ -\ 7 \\ \hline \end{array}$	36. $\begin{array}{r} 18 \\ -\ 8 \\ \hline \end{array}$
37. $\begin{array}{r} 17 \\ -\ 10 \\ \hline \end{array}$	38. $\begin{array}{r} 13 \\ -\ 7 \\ \hline \end{array}$	39. $\begin{array}{r} 15 \\ -\ 10 \\ \hline \end{array}$	40. $\begin{array}{r} 9 \\ +\ 16 \\ \hline \end{array}$	41. $\begin{array}{r} 8 \\ +\ 1 \\ \hline \end{array}$	42. $\begin{array}{r} 14 \\ -\ 8 \\ \hline \end{array}$
43. $\begin{array}{r} 9 \\ +\ 20 \\ \hline \end{array}$	44. $\begin{array}{r} 10 \\ +\ 6 \\ \hline \end{array}$	45. $\begin{array}{r} 19 \\ -\ 10 \\ \hline \end{array}$	46. $\begin{array}{r} 7 \\ +\ 0 \\ \hline \end{array}$	47. $\begin{array}{r} 16 \\ -\ 8 \\ \hline \end{array}$	48. $\begin{array}{r} 10 \\ +\ 19 \\ \hline \end{array}$
49. $\begin{array}{r} 15 \\ -\ 8 \\ \hline \end{array}$	50. $\begin{array}{r} 10 \\ +\ 1 \\ \hline \end{array}$	51. $\begin{array}{r} 9 \\ +\ 17 \\ \hline \end{array}$	52. $\begin{array}{r} 8 \\ +\ 4 \\ \hline \end{array}$	53. $\begin{array}{r} 8 \\ -\ 7 \\ \hline \end{array}$	54. $\begin{array}{r} 12 \\ -\ 7 \\ \hline \end{array}$
55. $\begin{array}{r} 13 \\ -\ 8 \\ \hline \end{array}$	56. $\begin{array}{r} 9 \\ +\ 7 \\ \hline \end{array}$	57. $\begin{array}{r} 16 \\ -\ 9 \\ \hline \end{array}$	58. $\begin{array}{r} 7 \\ +\ 17 \\ \hline \end{array}$	59. $\begin{array}{r} 7 \\ +\ 14 \\ \hline \end{array}$	60. $\begin{array}{r} 7 \\ +\ 12 \\ \hline \end{array}$

Day100

Adding and Subtracting

NAME: ___________   TIME: Score: /60

1. 13 − 10	2. 18 − 9	3. 13 − 7	4. 9 + 17	5. 9 + 14	6. 9 − 9
7. 19 − 8	8. 11 − 9	9. 11 − 8	10. 7 + 12	11. 8 + 8	12. 9 + 18
13. 16 − 8	14. 13 − 9	15. 10 + 6	16. 17 − 8	17. 19 − 9	18. 14 − 8
19. 8 + 16	20. 7 + 7	21. 8 − 8	22. 12 − 7	23. 9 + 20	24. 10 + 16
25. 9 + 9	26. 7 + 17	27. 8 + 11	28. 9 + 15	29. 18 − 8	30. 8 + 18
31. 9 + 10	32. 14 − 9	33. 9 + 7	34. 8 + 17	35. 16 − 10	36. 10 − 8
37. 9 + 16	38. 8 + 3	39. 8 + 1	40. 10 − 7	41. 15 − 8	42. 11 − 10
43. 8 + 6	44. 10 − 9	45. 9 − 8	46. 8 + 5	47. 13 − 8	48. 9 + 6
49. 8 + 14	50. 9 + 0	51. 11 − 7	52. 7 + 3	53. 16 − 9	54. 10 − 10
55. 20 − 10	56. 10 + 10	57. 20 − 8	58. 9 + 3	59. 14 − 7	60. 8 + 4

6 + 7	6 + 9	10 + 5	7 + 13	3 + 16	2 + 8
17 + 14	1 + 1	7 + 20	4 + 13	12 + 4	7 + 9
8 + 10	17 + 11	10 + 6	7 + 17	17 + 16	13 + 8
15 + 9	5 + 11	16 + 3	2 + 15	17 + 8	10 + 11
4 + 12	19 + 10	5 + 0	5 + 2	0 + 17	8 + 17
3 + 17	9 + 5	11 + 1	2 + 14	6 + 18	15 + 14
17 + 10	2 + 11	12 + 0	20 + 5	7 + 19	6 + 17
12 + 17	11 + 11	7 + 18	8 + 4	3 + 19	7 + 12
17 + 9	10 + 10	6 + 1	15 + 11	20 + 9	5 + 1
1 + 3	10 + 4	13 + 14	11 + 18	10 + 17	4 + 19

Day102

Adding and Subtracting

NAME: TIME: Score: /60

7 + 20	12 - 8	18 - 10	19 - 9	10 + 19	11 - 8
13 - 8	8 + 9	8 + 8	15 - 7	9 + 7	20 - 9
12 - 9	10 - 8	8 + 5	7 + 15	19 - 7	9 + 1
7 + 12	9 + 12	8 + 14	8 - 8	10 + 12	9 - 9
10 - 9	7 + 16	18 - 9	8 + 13	9 + 6	17 - 9
9 + 2	8 + 19	15 - 8	11 - 9	9 + 8	17 - 8
18 - 7	8 + 11	14 - 9	9 + 3	14 - 8	10 - 10
19 - 10	17 - 7	16 - 9	16 - 8	15 - 9	16 - 10
10 + 16	9 + 13	7 + 3	17 - 10	9 + 4	10 + 20
8 + 20	9 + 16	8 + 12	18 - 8	10 + 3	10 + 1

Day103

Adding and Subtracting

NAME: ___________   TIME: Score: /60

9 + 6	10 + 13	8 - 7	9 + 14	16 - 10	9 + 5
9 - 9	8 + 10	16 - 8	15 - 9	11 - 8	12 - 9
12 - 8	13 - 9	17 - 9	9 + 11	9 + 12	9 + 7
10 - 7	9 + 18	15 - 7	8 + 15	8 - 8	9 + 4
7 + 10	19 - 9	8 + 6	7 + 11	7 + 1	17 - 8
14 - 10	8 + 4	7 + 6	11 - 9	15 - 10	14 - 7
9 + 17	9 + 13	10 - 8	14 - 9	16 - 9	8 + 3
8 + 11	8 + 5	10 + 7	18 - 9	9 + 20	9 + 10
15 - 8	11 - 7	8 + 7	14 - 8	8 + 1	8 + 18
19 - 7	7 + 0	11 - 10	20 - 8	8 + 8	19 - 8

8 + 2	17 - 9	10 + 17	13 - 7	10 + 7	20 - 8
9 + 19	8 + 13	11 - 10	13 - 8	19 - 9	12 - 9
13 - 9	8 + 14	8 + 1	16 - 8	9 + 14	7 - 7
18 - 10	8 + 8	18 - 8	10 + 19	7 + 17	10 - 8
12 - 8	7 + 7	10 + 5	11 - 8	10 + 0	9 - 7
7 + 14	10 + 6	16 - 9	7 + 13	9 + 18	9 + 6
9 - 8	9 - 9	17 - 8	9 + 2	10 - 9	10 - 7
10 + 15	7 + 19	9 + 9	7 + 4	9 + 11	8 + 4
9 + 7	19 - 8	11 - 7	18 - 7	10 + 12	17 - 7
9 + 12	8 - 7	14 - 10	17 - 10	10 + 8	15 - 9

Day105

Adding and Subtracting

NAME: ______

TIME:

Score: /60

20 − 7	12 − 9	8 + 18	15 − 10	11 − 8	18 − 10
12 − 7	10 + 2	7 + 5	7 + 1	8 + 10	7 + 3
19 − 8	8 + 7	9 + 18	19 − 10	7 + 19	8 + 3
7 + 4	11 − 7	20 − 8	9 + 0	14 − 8	15 − 8
18 − 7	9 − 8	16 − 9	8 + 17	10 + 4	20 − 9
8 + 5	11 − 9	9 − 7	13 − 7	9 + 3	9 + 1
7 + 6	17 − 9	13 − 8	8 + 12	9 + 12	10 − 9
13 − 10	8 + 19	10 + 17	18 − 8	17 − 8	14 − 9
8 + 14	9 + 6	12 − 8	8 + 16	9 + 17	9 + 2
9 + 9	16 − 8	9 + 19	11 − 10	7 + 16	9 − 9

8 + 10	18 − 8	10 + 19	9 + 18	16 − 10	14 − 8
12 − 9	18 − 9	8 + 11	19 − 9	19 − 10	7 + 10
9 + 15	16 − 8	8 + 14	7 + 5	10 − 9	20 − 10
8 + 1	14 − 10	11 − 9	9 + 10	9 + 11	9 + 12
7 + 6	10 + 20	10 + 18	9 + 1	9 − 8	7 + 12
8 + 17	8 + 15	12 − 10	16 − 7	17 − 10	7 + 19
18 − 10	15 − 9	9 + 16	17 − 8	14 − 9	10 − 7
20 − 7	9 − 7	8 + 7	15 − 10	7 + 1	8 − 8
19 − 8	17 − 7	8 + 8	9 + 8	9 + 9	11 − 10
9 + 14	9 − 9	9 + 7	17 − 9	7 + 11	9 + 19

12 − 8	19 − 9	11 − 7	14 − 9	8 − 8	16 − 9
13 − 7	13 − 10	9 + 7	7 + 16	9 + 10	20 − 7
8 + 20	9 − 8	9 + 9	8 + 2	10 + 2	11 − 8
16 − 8	8 − 7	8 + 16	7 + 3	9 + 4	9 + 13
8 + 4	18 − 8	9 + 2	15 − 8	8 + 17	7 + 2
9 + 18	17 − 10	11 − 10	8 + 13	13 − 8	10 + 7
19 − 7	9 + 1	12 − 9	9 + 19	9 + 3	10 − 10
9 − 7	8 + 5	19 − 8	10 − 8	18 − 10	13 − 9
7 + 12	10 + 19	10 + 1	8 + 1	8 + 12	8 + 9
7 + 1	9 + 5	9 − 9	10 − 9	16 − 7	17 − 7

Day108

Adding and Subtracting

NAME: TIME: Score: /60

8 + 5	9 + 12	15 - 8	8 + 19	10 - 7	12 - 9
10 + 18	9 - 7	12 - 10	7 + 8	10 + 1	10 + 4
10 - 8	13 - 7	8 + 1	8 + 11	8 + 4	14 - 10
14 - 8	11 - 8	16 - 8	8 + 15	7 + 20	18 - 8
9 + 13	19 - 9	15 - 9	10 + 12	8 + 2	9 - 9
8 + 12	12 - 8	13 - 9	12 - 7	13 - 8	7 + 17
17 - 7	8 - 7	7 + 7	18 - 9	9 + 15	7 + 19
10 - 10	9 + 9	17 - 9	7 + 0	7 + 15	8 - 8
7 + 4	20 - 10	9 + 6	14 - 9	19 - 7	10 - 9
8 + 6	20 - 8	10 + 10	8 + 0	9 + 17	8 + 7

10 + 0	19 − 8	16 − 10	14 − 8	10 − 9	14 − 9
10 + 19	10 + 1	8 + 1	7 + 16	16 − 7	8 + 4
9 + 1	13 − 8	13 − 7	11 − 10	8 + 16	8 + 19
9 − 8	8 + 11	10 − 8	7 + 14	20 − 10	11 − 9
15 − 9	8 + 12	7 + 13	9 − 7	19 − 9	15 − 10
14 − 7	8 + 9	9 + 2	13 − 10	19 − 10	8 + 6
16 − 9	11 − 8	11 − 7	7 + 7	9 + 14	10 + 10
8 + 7	17 − 7	7 + 2	8 + 5	9 + 7	10 + 5
14 − 10	17 − 10	20 − 8	15 − 8	9 + 10	9 + 11
12 − 8	9 + 3	12 − 9	9 + 0	9 + 19	10 + 4